Change Forces with a Vengeance

Change Forces with a Vengeance is the third book in the chaos theory trilogy (now called complexity theory). The first two books focused on understanding the real complexity of educational reform in action. This book pushes even deeper by providing new insights and lessons of change concerning moral purpose, and what is called tri-level reform – the school and community, the local district and the state. It draws on reform initiatives across many levels and countries so that the ideas are grounded in the reality of actual projects and findings as the forces of change play themselves out within and across the three levels.

Changing Forces with a Vengeance is different from the previous two books in one major respect. Instead of being content with understanding complex system dynamics, it takes up the more daunting question of how systems can be changed for the better. It is a humbling proposition because systems don't change all that easily, and complexity theory is the operative paradigm which means that systems can only be 'guided', not 'managed'. By stretching the limits of how the educational system can be changed for the better, exciting new possibilities are identified: what new horizons should we be striving for to improve learning for all children? How can we achieve large-scale reform and do it in a way that the conditions for sustainability are enhanced? What policy levers are needed, and what is the role of new leadership in accomplishing sustainable, comprehensive reform? These questions and more are addressed in ways that are both deeply theoretical, and powerfully practical.

Michael Fullan is the Dean of the Ontario Institute for Studies in Education at the University of Toronto. He is recognized as an international authority on educational reform. He is engaged in training, consulting and evaluation of change projects around the world. His ideas for managing change are used in many countries and his books have been published in several languages. His *What's Worth Fighting For* trilogy (with Andy Hargreaves), *Change Forces* triology, *The New Meaning of Educational Change* and *Leading in a Culture of Change* are widely acclaimed. *Leading in a Culture of Change* won the book of the year award in 2002 from the national Staff Development Council, USA

Related Titles

Change Forces: Probing the Depths of Educational Reform
Michael Fullan

Change Forces: The Sequel
Michael Fullan

School Leadership and Complexity Theory
Keith Morrison

Leading Learners, Leading Schools
Robin Brooke-Smith

Change Forces with a Vengeance

Michael Fullan

RoutledgeFalmer
Taylor & Francis Group

LONDON AND NEW YORK

First published 2003
by RoutledgeFalmer
11 New Fetter Lane, London EC4P 4EE

Simultaneously published in the USA and Canada
by RoutledgeFalmer
29 West 35th Street, New York, NY 10001

RoutledgeFalmer is an imprint of the Taylor & Francis Group

Typeset in Garamond
by HWA Text and Data Management, Tunbridge Wells
Printed and bound in the USA by
Sheridan Books, Ann Arbor, Michigan

British Library Cataloguing in Publication Data
A catalogue record for this book is available from the British
Library

Library of Congress Cataloging in Publication Data
Fullan, Michael.
        Change forces with a vengeance / Michael Fullan.
        p. cm.
    Includes bibliographical references and index.
        1. Educational change. 2. Educational planning. I. Title

    LB2806 .F793 2003
    371.2–dc21

                                                          2002023993

ISBN 0–415–23084–5 (hbk)
ISBN 0–415–23085–3 (pbk)

Praise for Michael Fullan and *Change Forces with a Vengeance*

This excellent book reveals that Michael Fullan has learnt much from our reform in England as we have learnt from him. *Change Forces with a Vengeance* is a fascinating account at the cutting edge of large scale change.

Michael Barber
Head, Policy Delivery Unit
Prime Minister Tony Blair's Office, United Kingdom

Change Forces with a Vengeance focuses and deepens our knowledge about large-scale change and improvement in public schools. It leads us into the big questions of how large-scale improvement can be made understandable and tractable, and how the institutional context of public schooling can be changed to support powerful learning for students and teachers.

Richard F. Elmore
Gregory R. Anrig Professor of Educational Leadership
Graduate School of Education, Harvard University

Michael Fullan, the world maestro of educational change shows not only how to make change stick but also how to make it spread and last. Cutting edge and controversial as ever, Fullan lets no teacher, leader or government rest on their educational laurels.

Andy Hargreaves
Thomas More Brennan Chair in Education
Department of Teacher Education, Curriculum and Instruction
Lynch School of Education, Boston College

In *Change Forces With a Vengeance* Fullan provides a comprehensive analysis of the complexity of large-scale reform together with insights as how to manage it. Fullan's book is enormously helpful. He not only delivers his characteristic insights and action oriented syntheses of the research, but also and more importantly, gives us the inspiration and courage to continue.

Professor David Hopkins
Head of the Standards and Effectiveness Unit
Department for Education and Skills, United Kingdom

Michael Fullan continues to push the envelope of understanding about the change process. With deep insight, he rejects the notion that the larger context in which change efforts take place, is a "state of affairs" or a given that must be understood rather than tampered with. Armed with a commitment to moral purpose and practical examples from his vast on-the-ground experience, Fullan points the way to sustainable transformation in education and beyond.

Dr Charles E. Pascal
Executive Director, Atkinson Charitable Foundation and
Former Ontario Deputy Minister of Education

No one involved in education at this time should miss reading this book. Significant change is needed to prepare our children to deal with the knowledge era. This is not the blueprint but the best guide that we have. It is not possible to ignore this book.

Steve Stanley
Director, Centre for Excellence in Teaching
Fremantle, Western Australia

In this extraordinary book, Michael Fullan hits us squarely with forceful, ground-breaking truth. He is a master at packing ideational density into each sentence. Insight and heart meet up with the power of words. Fullan understands the complexity of sustainable large-scale change as few others do. His words give us a clear, concise, power-packed charge of what we must do if we aim to achieve deeper transferability and sustainable system change. Beautifully written, this book is a must-read for all whoa re serious about being in the business of education.

Alice Thomas
Founder, President and CEO, Center for Development and Learning
Covington, LA

With profound insights and practical wisdom *Change Forces with a Vengeance* gives hope and inspiration that real change is not only possible but achievable in our schools. Michael Fullan shows that sustainable system-wide change cannot happen without passion, knowledge, and the courage to change the context in which teachers and students work and learn. For anyone who cares passionately about the future of public education, this is a must read book.

Rick Lash
National Director for Management Development
The HAYGROUP, Canada

Michael Fullan challenges everyone engaged in educational reform to go down a road not yet traveled because it is not yet made—large scale change in whole system contexts. *Change Forces with a Vengeance* shows why facilitative system contexts are imperative for educational reform and invites us on "an intellectual journey of the highest order." This exciting book moves the field to a new under-standing of what deep, sustainable reform will take and offers grounded advice about how to get there. It is masterful.

Milbrey McLaughlin
David Jacks Professor of Education and Public Policy
Stanford University

Change Forces With a Vengeance is essential reading for anyone interested in school improvement, leadership and learning. It is extremely well written, timely and evocative. Extraordinarily effective.

John Bransford
Learning Technology Center, Vanderbilt University, USA

For Matt and Michael
Male muses

Contents

List of Figures

Preface

Change Forces With a Vengeance is the third book in a second set of trilogies. The evolution is important. The first series — *What's Worth Fighting For* — provided advice for principals and teachers in coping with difficult circumstances (Fullan, 1997; Fullan and Hargreaves, 1992; and Hargreaves and Fullan, 1998). If one looks closely at *What's Worth Fighting For*, the underlying premise was that on any given day the larger "system" may not know what it is doing. Therefore, we argued, don't count on the system but rather carve out your own niche of effectiveness working with others. Our guidelines were in support of this mind and action set. Not a very optimistic orientation on our part, but a practical one.

As I turned to the *Change Forces* trilogy, the attention shifted directly to the system. Using chaos theory (now called complexity theory) as applied to social systems, I tried to make sense of the real complexity of larger entities in action. In the first two books, the emphasis was on *understanding* complexity with a view to coping more effectively with non-linear reform (Fullan, 1993, 1999). *Change Forces With a Vengeance* represents a significant shift. It still focuses on the system and still strives for deeper understanding but inserts a new question: What would the larger system look like if it did know what it was doing?

Put another way, instead of treating the larger context as a given, we start to focus on *changing* the context. The context becomes a dependent variable — something to affect for the better. It is a humbling proposition. Contexts don't change that easily and complexity theory is the operative paradigm which means that systems can't be "managed" and that reforms rarely unfold as intended.

It has become imperative, however, to attempt to affect substantial system change because without the latter you cannot get large-scale, sustainable reform. The focus on large-scale reform became evident in the 1990s. Policymakers became more earnest in their attempt to improve whole systems (districts, states). About the turn of the century many of us have added sustainability because deeper, more lasting reform is not possible without paying attention to establishing the conditions for continuous reform.

This is an exciting proposition. The stakes are high, the risk is great, the breakthroughs and the yield could be enormously beneficial to society. Fortunately, empirical examples of deliberate attempts at large-scale reform are multiplying, which provides us with living laboratories in which strategizing and inquiry go hand in hand. My colleagues and I rarely do distant research any more. All of our current initiatives are large-scale, developmental, multi-year partnerships with school districts, state departments, provinces and entire countries, and they are taking place around the world. We are applying knowledge as we create it. We are creating knowledge as we apply it. We are changing systems from top to bottom; not in deep ways yet, but the attempts have never been so purposeful and informed. Our partners are increasingly teachers, administrators, policymakers.

All the ideas in this book come from working with others. There are simply too many people to thank by name. Even the number of formal projects is too great to name. The great advantage we have is the different modes of learning that feed into each other. Sometimes it is multi-year training and in-depth workshops, and while it may appear that the training is one-way, you cannot spend 100 hours over the course of a year with a given group of school and district teams without learning more than you give. Other times, it is critical friend consultancies in which you grapple with complex problems in order to tease out ideas that lead to further development in the situation. Still others include evaluation research where we consolidate knowledge while pushing the strategy envelope.

I thank all my academic and field-based colleagues for the learning and hope that they have given over the years. The ideas in this book have been developed collectively with this or that individual, team or larger group. I once heard a reply to a charge of plagiarism, where the author's defense was "my memory disguised itself as my imagination." I do not want to claim imaginative insights, but rather to acknowledge that this book is a tribute to our collective memory — a memory that is ever-wise, ever-reflective and ever-active.

I would like to thank Malcolm Clarkson for initiating the *Change Forces* trilogy and Anna Clarkson of RoutledgeFalmer for her continuing support of the *Change Forces* trilogy.

As with all the books, my deep gratitude goes to Claudia Cuttress who produced the manuscript.

I ended *Change Forces: The Sequel* with the following reference to unfinished business:

Those engaged in education reform are those engaged in societal development; those engaged in societal development are those engaged in the evolution of virtue. It is time to return to large-scale reform with even more ambitious goals ... armed with the knowledge that we can turn complexity's own hidden power to our advantage. (p. 84)

Sustainable system change is the agenda, and we are at the very early stages of an exciting journey.

Chapter 1

New Horizons

You know that the more magnificent the prospect, the lesser the certainty, and also the greater the passion.

Freud

Chapters 1 and 2 are twinned. This chapter concerns scale, scope and *intellectual* depth. Chapter 2 adds *moral* substance. The synergy of intellectual and moral forces would be unbeatable except we are far from establishing the conditions for this to happen. But we are making progress and gaining a clearer understanding of what remains to be done.

I start with the case of educational reform in England. A word of explanation: The United Kingdom consists of four separate educational departments — England, Wales, Scotland, and Northern Ireland. I focus here only on the recent reforms in England.

To illustrate what I mean by "new horizons" I will identify a first level of accomplishment, only to be followed by the realization that there are richer horizons that lay beyond. At the time of writing, late 2002, we are in the final year of a four-year evaluation of the National Literacy and Numeracy Strategy in England (Earl *et al.*, 2003). NLNS is the most ambitious large-scale reform initiative anywhere in the world. Baseline measures were established in England in 1996 using the performance of 11-year-olds in literacy and numeracy as the initial markers. A comprehensive top-down strategy was then orchestrated which invested in accountability mechanisms and capacity-building (professional development, quality instructional materials, new leadership roles) (see Barber, 2001). A team of us at the University of Toronto was contracted to monitor these efforts and to feed back our assessment on an ongoing basis of how well the process was doing and how it could be improved.

Government leaders announced four-year targets and committed to their achievement. In particular, the baseline measures indicated that in 1996, 57 percent of 11-year-olds were achieving acceptable proficiency in literacy, and 54 percent were so doing in numeracy. The targets for 2002 announced in 1997 were 80 percent for literacy and 75 percent in numeracy. The Secretary of State for Education and Employment, David Blunkett, said that he would resign his post as minister if the targets were not attained (he is, of course, no longer minister, being promoted largely because of his success in education).

This is large-scale reform. There are 19,000 primary schools involved. In effect, the government set out to improve the vast majority of schools in the system, at least as far as literacy and numeracy are concerned, within a four-year period. The results at the end of the initial reform period, 2002, are displayed in Figure 1.1. While the targets were not met the results are impressive. Literacy achievement has improved from 57 percent to 75 percent, having leveled off the last two years. The main reasons for the shortfall are that writing lagged behind reading and girls outperformed boys. Greater attention is being paid to both these components in current strategies. Mathematics scores increased from 54 percent to 73 percent just short of the 75 percent target. These are remarkable achievements across a large, complex system. (I raise a more fundamental question shortly as to whether centrally-driven strategies eventually run out of steam.)

This is not the place to discuss all the ins and outs of the strategy. There are debates about possible side effects such as burnout, loss of creativity, and some questions about the validity of some of the measures in literacy. As evaluators, we have no doubt, however, that literacy and numeracy have improved substantially in England over the four-year period. In Chapter 2 I will add some impressive data on the moral question of closing the gap between high and low performers.

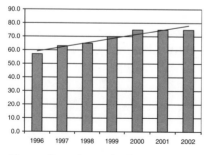

Literacy: Percentage at level 4 or above

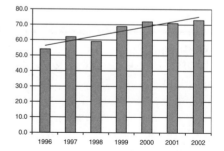

Numeracy: Percentage at Level 4 or above

Figure 1.1 Results of school reform in England (DfEE, 2002)

In any case, I am going to call the large-scale improvement of literacy and numeracy "new horizon #1." We will see the same improvement in school districts in the United States (see Chapter 5). In other words, over the last five or so years we have learned how to improve literacy and numeracy in large systems (school districts, and in the case of England, a country). More work needs to be done, but these are, indeed, impressive improvements.

Despite these accomplishments, which most of us would have said could not be done within a five-year period, I will now argue that these changes are not deep, only first steps in terms of the deeper reforms that are required for the twenty-first century. Here we turn to "new horizon #2" to talk about the substance of what lies ahead. I will use four examples: the England case, a study of the implementation of new mathematics in California, some hard questions posed by Richard Elmore about the limitations of current practice in schools, and improvement of the teaching profession in Connecticut.

A curious thing happened in England during what I will call Phase I reform (1997–2002). As literacy and numeracy scores rose, the morale of teachers and principals, if anything, declined. I believe that the reason for this is (a) the basic working conditions of teachers did not change to enable them to become fully engaged, and (b) the literacy and numeracy strategies, *per se*, were not actually aimed at altering this more fundamental situation.

Put another way, literacy and numeracy improvements are real, but only a first step. Engaged students, energetic and committed teachers, improvements in problem-solving and thinking skills, greater emotional intelligence, and, generally, teaching and learning for deeper understanding cannot be orchestrated from the center (although as we shall see, the center has a crucial but different role). High-powered learning environments which are intensively learner-centered, knowledge-centered and assessment-centered require great capacities and commitment from the entire teaching force and its leadership, and thus will require different strategies from the ones currently employed to address literacy and numeracy (see Bransford, Brown and Cocking, 1999).

Based partly on our criticism that Phase I strategies had almost reached their limit and partly on the government's own concern that more fundamental transformation was required if teachers were to be fully engaged, English policymakers are now grappling with the question of what should be the policy set for Phase II reform. One of their initial formulations is extremely helpful in viewing new horizon questions in historical perspective (Figure 1.2).

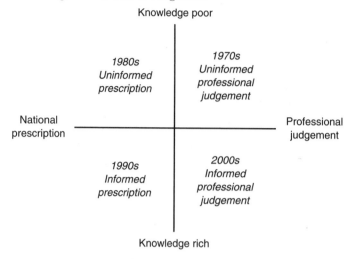

Figure 1.2 Knowledge poor–rich, prescription–judgment matrix (Barber, 2002)

Crossing knowledge poor–rich with prescription–judgment, the evolution of reform strategies over the past four decades is neatly and generally accurately portrayed. Prior to accountability and in the days of loosely coupled professional individualism, the 1970s is seen as "uninformed professional judgment." External ideas did not easily find their way into schools, and even if they existed or got there they did not flow across classrooms. There was little quality control of innovations that were attempted although there were pockets of productive collaboration through teacher centers in the 1960s and 1970s.

Growing concerns with the performance and accountability of school systems, marked in the United States in 1986 by *A Nation at Risk*, resulted in a set of state driven prescriptions for reform which can be accurately described as the "uninformed prescription" of the 1980s and beyond. There may have been standards and goals (even these in many cases were ill-conceived), but there was virtually the complete absence of any capacity-building strategies and resources for how to get there.

Concerned with national or state-driven reforms, some entities like England moved into a more carefully considered era of "informed prescription" in the 1990s. Mind you, the label is debatable in two respects. There remained the majority of states and nations that were not exercising *informed* prescription. And for those that claimed they were, again England, who says they were informed? Nonetheless, there was a deliberate process to base policies and practices on the best of research and knowledge, and further, to continually refine prescriptions through further research and inquiry.

Informed prescription, the argument goes, can take us to the first horizon, but not much further. For deeper developments we need the creative energies and ownership of the teaching force and its leaders. Hence, the current emphasis on "informed professional judgment."

These formulations are exceedingly helpful as an overview but there are several key questions. First, does a decade of informed prescription create the preconditions for moving to informed professional judgment, or does it actually inhibit it by fostering external dependency? Second, is there the danger in moving to informed professional judgment that the gains of valuable prescription will slip away? Put another way, did informed prescription actually hamper the creativities of teachers, or did it rein in a range of permissive but highly questionable practice that went under the name of creativity and autonomy? Third, how do you move, anyway, from prescription to autonomy? We might be able to portray what informed professional judgment might look like but the *pathways* for getting there will be enormously complex and different depending on the starting point. For example, if trust, morally purposeful policy, coherence, capacity, knowledge management and continuous innovation are conditions for collectively informed professional judgment, how do you establish these "facilitative system conditions"?

The point is not to answer these questions right now, but rather to say that we are finally getting somewhere. Part of this development is to begin to focus more on the system and policy levers in order to alter the working and learning conditions in schools (see Chapter 6). For example, the British government commissioned PriceWaterhouse Coopers (2001) to study the working conditions of teachers and head teachers (in their own right and in comparison to business and industry). PWC concluded that if the goals of the educational system are to be realized:

> An essential strand will be to reduce teacher workload, foster increased teacher ownership, and create the capacity to manage change in a sustainable way that can lay the foundation for improved school and pupil performance in the future. (p. 2)

The horizon question, of course, is how do you foster widespread teacher ownership? But it is still the right question and establishes the agenda as it should be. In Chapter 6 we will return to the role of policy with the point that the policies and strategies which were successful in Phase I (i.e., improving literacy and numeracy) will not be the ones required to go beyond Phase I. David Hargreaves (2002: 2–3) makes this very case in talking about "tests for creative policy-makers" such as a *new levers test*:

> Many initiatives have taken the form of a new lever that has worked well. But all levers have their limits. Educational processes are very complex, affected by many variables, so the amount of improvement any single lever can effect is smaller than reformers might wish. Moreover, when a new lever has demonstrable positive impact, policymakers have a tendency to push the lever beyond its limits. For example, in England, "targets" — for students teachers, schools, local education authorities — have had a real effect on raising standards, but because targets have worked, policymakers demand yet more of them. The danger, of course, is that this can induce resistance to the very notion of a target and thus ruin what was originally a very effective lever. Rather than pushing an old lever beyond its natural limits, policymakers would be wise to search for new levers. So the new levers test asks: *Has this reform reached its natural limits and should a new lever be sought to complement or replace it?* (emphasis in original)

Developing new levers is a challenge of the highest order because it must result in unleashing energy, commitment, resources and learning on a very large scale to accomplish thing never done before.

Three additional cases in point illustrate the scope of this challenge. First is Cohen and Hill's (2001) study of California's decade-long effort to change and improve mathematics teaching. Their conclusion is stated up front:

> The policy was a success for some California teachers and students. It led to the creation of new opportunities for teachers to learn, rooted either in improved student curriculum or in examples of students' work or the state assessment or both. Teachers were able to work together on serious problems of curriculum teaching and learning in short-term professional communities. The policy also helped to create coherence among elements of the curriculum, assessment, and learning opportunities for certain teachers. Such coherence is quite rare in the blizzard of often divergent guidance for instruction that typically blows over U.S. public schools. Only a modest fraction of California elementary teachers — *roughly 10 percent — had the experiences just summarized.* (p. 9, emphasis added)

Cohen and Hill argue that three "policy instruments," in combination, resulted in improvements: curriculum, assessment, and teacher learning:

> The things that make a difference to changes in their practice were integral to instruction: curricular materials for teachers and students to use in classes; assessments that enabled students to demonstrate their mathematical performance — and teachers to consider it — and instruction for teachers that was grounded in these curriculum materials and assessment. (p. 6)

Cohen and Hill also found that norms of collaboration among teachers were generally weak, and that collaboration *per se* does not mean that new ideas would necessarily flourish. This requires explanations and leads to a more useful merging of our prescription/ judgment combination. Cohen and Hill again:

> Stronger and more broadly supported professional norms of collabo- ration were associated with conventional ideas [in mathematics], an outcome that shows that professional communities can be conservative as well as progressive … Professional contexts are likely to bear on teachers' ideas and practices only when they create or actively support teachers' learning of matters closely related to instruction, and most professional collegiality and community in American schools is at present disconnected from such learning … The key point is that the *content* of teacher learning matters. (pp. 11–12, emphasis in original)

Now we are getting somewhere. While Cohen and Hill may rely too heavily on "the informed prescription" of (in this case) mathematics reformers, the conclusion is the same. Let us focus on what we mean by "informed" and not make the error of relying solely on professional communities, or for that matter on external expertise. *Both* are required, i.e., reforms need to be pursued under conditions which maximize intensive teacher learning, involving external ideas as well as internal ideas, interaction and judgment.

In building professional learning communities, Andy Hargreaves (2003) reminds us that this is not a straightforward matter. He makes the point that many versions of apparent professional learning communities are actually quite superficial and narrow. Hargreaves claims that teachers and schools in poorer communities are being subjected to a form of performance training that provides intensive implementation support but only in relation to highly prescriptive interventions. He worries that it will be difficult to move beyond standardization into productive professional learning communities.

In any case, in California productive learning only occurred for about one in ten teachers. The good news is that the California reformers never deliberately designed their efforts to have maximum impact. Thus the potential for greater impact could be realized by better policies (see Chapter 6). Equally problematic, as Cohen and Hill observe, is that there was no built-in attempt to learn and improve policy levers as you go; an essential requirement for large-scale reform:

> Policymakers and reformers in California were not well informed about the effects of their endeavors; they made no attempt to learn systematically about how the reforms played out in schools and classrooms. As a result, they had no evidence to inform either their work or public debate. (p. 187)

Another telling case in point is Richard Elmore's (2002a) "hard questions about practice": "people who work in schools do not pay attention to the connection between how they organize and manage themselves and how they take care of their own and their students learning" (p. 22). He continues:

> The idea behind distributed leadership is that the complex nature of instructional practice requires people to operate in networks of shared and complementary expertise rather than in hierarchies ... The schools that I have observed usually share a strong motivation to learn new teaching practices and a sense of urgency about improving learning for students and teachers. What they lack is a sense of individual and collective agency, or control, over the organizational conditions that affect the learning of students and adults in their schools. (p. 24)

A third and different case is Connecticut's successful efforts to improve teaching and learning through new teaching polices (Wilson, Darling-Hammond and Berry, 2001):

> The Connecticut case is a story of how bipartisan state policymakers initiated and sustained a coherent policy package linking school finance reform equalization and challenging expectations for students to teacher salary increases, teacher licensing and re-certification reforms, and a teacher support and assessment system guided by student and teaching standards. Rather than pursue a single silver bullet or change strategies every few years, Connecticut made ongoing investments in improving teaching through high standards

and high supports and a coherent connection to student learning
... Large, steady gains in student achievement and a plentiful supply
of well-qualified teachers are two major outcomes of this agenda.
(p. 4)

We return to this case in Chapter 6, but recognize it now as an
example of sustained policy coherence, and constant refinement
through learning from experience. It is an example of "informed
prescription" and thus does not go far enough. For example, the
deep learning on the job, as envisaged by Cohen and Hill, and Elmore,
that would be evidenced in the transformation of working conditions
is not the direct focus of Connecticut's policy. They take us to one
new horizon, but not beyond.

What can we say, then, about some of the characteristics of new
horizons? First, they are large-scale, having a "systemness" quality;
they attempt to alter the system. In this sense I do not consider
comprehensive school-wide reform models, such as "Success for All"
to meet the large-scale system criterion. Even though they may be in
several thousand schools they are not centrally involved in changing
entire systems. We need to change the latter in order to go to new
horizons.

Second, what appears to be a valuable new horizon — improving
literacy and numeracy for the vast majority of students in the system
— turns out to be only a first order accomplishment. First steps in the
big scheme of things.

Third, ultimate horizons have to do with deeper transformation
and sustainability. No one is there yet and no one has seriously
attempted it (but some are poised). In this scenario we see *collective*
informed professional judgment flourishing. Knowledge, ideas and
breakthroughs around more fundamental cognitive and affective
learning goals are constantly being pursued, scrutinized, and refined.

At the same time, we see that this scenario is a far cry from where
we are now. In this chapter I have tried to make the case that this is
an intellectual journey of the highest order. It is large and complex
and will require the best ideas along the way. While great ideas will
be necessary, and even tremendously exciting, the task is too large
and will require almost superhuman effort over a sustained period.
There is a missing force so far and that is moral purpose and passion.
If one examines the Connecticut reform or, in England, the recent
speech by Estelle Morris, then Secretary of State for Education and
Skills, the emphasis, rightly, is on upgrading the profession. She
identified six characteristics of the modern profession:

1. High standards at the levels of the profession, including entry and leadership, set nationally and regulated by a strong professional body.
2. A body of knowledge about what works and why, with regular training and development opportunities so that members of the profession are always up to date.
3. Efficient organization and management of complementary staff to support best professional practice.
4. Effective use of leading edge technology to support best professional practice.
5. Incentives and rewards for excellence, including pay structure.
6. A relentless focus on what is in the best interest of those who use the service — in education, pupils and parents — backed by clear and effective arrangements for accountability and for measuring performance and outcomes. (Morris, 2001:3)

A good agenda, to be sure, but what is missing from this list is the purpose and passion that drives the best teachers. We don't need the isolated passion of individual teachers. We need a modern version which includes, but goes beyond, the individual. It is larger, more collective where individuals are motivated to make their own day-to-day contribution, while at the same time seeing themselves connected to others, not just locally, but beyond. It is, in a word, "moral purpose writ large" which as it turns out is both a goal in its own right, and equally importantly, a vital means to reach new horizons.

Chapter 2

Moral Purpose Writ Large

With all the emphasis on uninformed and informed prescription over the past twenty years, one of the casualties has been teachers' intrinsic motivation or sense of moral purpose. Over a quarter of a century ago, Dan Lortie (1975), identified "psychic rewards" as the source of greatest motivation and satisfaction among teachers. In his study of 6,000 teachers, Lortie found that these psychic rewards, "the times I reached a student or group of students and they have learned" were valued by 5,000 of the 6,000 teachers as a source of great gratification. The next most frequent response — respect from others — was selected by 2,100.

To this day, Parker Palmer (1998) talks about the *Courage to Teach* as teaching from the "Heart of Hope." He and his colleagues call for teachers to revisit their moral purpose by asking themselves the following questions:

> Why did I become a teacher in the first place?
> What do I stand for as a teacher?
> What are the gifts I bring to my work?
> What do I want my legacy to be?
> What can I do to "keep track of myself" — to remember my own heart? (Livsey with Palmer, 1999:16)

Policymakers and others have to find ways to reintroduce this source of motivation into the new horizons agenda. To a certain extent much is to be gained by stressing and valuing the moral purpose of teachers in making a difference in the lives of students but this will not be sufficient, and in fact, is not the main point of this chapter. Even in its heyday, probably only a minority of teachers operated with great moral purpose over their careers. Moreover, individual teachers trying to make a difference here and there could never achieve a great impact twenty-five years ago let alone in the complexities of twenty-first century living and learning.

Instead, I am suggesting that moral purpose must go beyond the individual; must be larger and more collective in nature. Indeed, I will claim that the only measure that counts at the end of the day is whether the *gap* between high and low performers is explicitly reduced. This result is more profound for societal development than most people realize. Let's consider some of the findings and their consequences as we move from the small picture (the classroom) through the school, the district, across districts, and across states and nations.

First, within the classroom, teachers must strive to reach all or the vast majority of the range of students. This usually does not happen, especially in high schools. Ken Dryden (1995) spent a year observing in classrooms in a Canadian high school. He notes, "so much is going on in each kid's life, every story is so complicated" (p. 84). Students are often disengaged from their own learning and it is enormously difficult for teachers to enter their world. Many teachers, reports Dryden, end up, metaphorically speaking, teaching "to the front row," reaching ten or fewer students in a class of thirty.

Similarly, at both the classroom and school level, McLaughlin and Talbert's (2001) detailed study of 16 high schools revealed three patterns of teaching practice:

1. Enacting traditions of practice
2. Lowering expectations and standards
3. Innovating to engage learners. (p. 19)

It was only the third pattern which increased success with lower performing students. Moreover, when they focused on professional learning communities (teachers working together) they found first that there wasn't much of it in evidence. And second, when strong teacher communities did exist they tended to be of two types: traditional communities, in which teachers in effect interacted to reinforce each other's ineffective practice thereby increasing the gap between high and low performers; or teacher learning communities, in which teachers collaborate to reinvent practice in order to reach all students (p. 62).

Sticking with the school level these findings take on critical importance in light of recent research on effective schools. Most school improvement efforts focus on improving schools and use aggregate school data as evidence (in a moment I will say that this should still be done). Research, however, sometimes shows that classroom-to-classroom variation in student performance is greater within schools than it is across schools. Doug Wilms (2001) found this in his study of New Brunswick schools in Canada:

> The finding of greatest importance ... is that there is considerably more variation at the classroom level than at the school level. In other words, results tend to vary more from class to class within schools than they do from school to school within districts. (pp. 6–7)

This means that strategies of development must be in the service of particular teachers within schools, not simply of entire schools. Put another way, professional learning communities within schools are important because they can reduce intra-school variation (see Chapter 4).

Again, with schools, Wilms found that "schools that were successful — those that had high average growth rates — did so mainly by increasing the growth rates of low ability students. High ability students tended to do well in every school" (pp. 10–11). In other words, they focused on reducing the gap.

At the risk of becoming bogged down in the research, we need to add the recent sophisticated PISA study (Programme for International Student Assessment) from the OECD (OECD, 2000). Over 265,000 15-year-olds in 32 countries were given independent performance assessments in reading, mathematics and science. This research provides a more nuanced picture. In countries which stream students by types of school (e.g., Austria, Belgium, Germany) between school differences are greater than within school differences. Conversely, in countries with less school segregation (e.g., New Zealand, Norway, Canada) the differences are mainly within schools.

The main point is that *context matters* more than individual background (and it is possible to alter the former):

> The socio-economic composition of a school's student population is an even stronger predictor than individual home background. PISA shows, for example, that two students with the same family characteristics going to different schools — one with a higher and one with a lower socio-economic profile — could expect to be further apart in reading literacy than two students from different backgrounds going to the same school. (p. 21)

I am not saying that individual teachers can influence all contexts, but I am saying that teachers, administrators and policymakers alike must alter context (within the classroom, across classrooms within the school, and across schools) in order to reduce the gap between high and low performers, and to reduce the gap they must explicitly monitor the gap reduction (not just overall achievement trends), and take appropriate action.

This is not as far-fetched as it sounds and we must return to England to make the point. Recall Figure 1.2 that revealed overall increases in literacy and numeracy achievement over the 1996–2002 period. Now let's use another measure which compares district (Local Education Authority — LEA) scores (Figure 2.1).

Figure 2.1 is the same measure as in Figure 1.1 (the percentage of 11-year-olds achieving proficiency in mathematics) but aggregated to the district (LEA) level. The graph shows that in 1998 there was at least one district that had only 40 percent of its 11-year-olds doing well enough, and at least one with 75 percent of its students performing at this level (a range of 35 percentage points). By 2000, the lowest average district was 61 percent and the highest 80 percent (a 19 point spread). This is a prime example of focusing on gap closing by raising the bar for all as one reduces the gap.

Figure 2.1 compares districts and we need, as I have already said, to disaggregate at all levels: across schools within districts, within schools, and within classrooms as well as within ethnic, gender and poverty groups. Several more concrete examples of within district gap closing come from England.

The headline in the June 21, 2002 issue of the *Times Educational Supplement* from England blares (pardon the pun): "Poorest children close results gap." It goes on to report "poverty-stricken districts in some of the largest cities have registered staggering gains in national test scores for 11-year-olds since 1997, far outstripping national

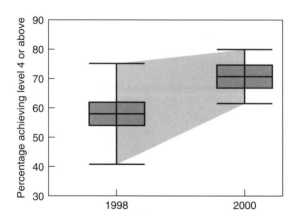

Figure 2.1 England: distribution of LEA results

increases" (p. 1). Overall, the report continues, "the gap between the scores of pupils in England's poorest 10 wards and the national average has closed by a third in the past five years." In 1997, in literacy, the gap between the ten poorest areas and the national average was 66 points (on a scale which ranged from 0 to 150). By 2002, the gap was 43 points. These gains are a result of a deliberate strategy to "raise the bar and close the gap" by investing in better teaching and raising standards — investing across the board, but disproportionably higher in poor areas which have farther to go and have less capacity to get there.

In the same issue, the accomplishments of Birmingham Local Education Authority are celebrated. The largest district in England with 659 schools, 178,000 pupils and 8,000 teachers, Birmingham has doubled the number of 11-year-olds achieving proficiency in literacy over the five-year period 1997–2002.

There are still significant gaps so this does not solve the problem; and literacy is just the beginning. But we are achieving movement on a scale never before seen and it is being done purposely through policies and strategy.

The PISA study also demonstrates how important it is to focus on gaps as well as overall achievement. If one simply compares countries by overall (average) achievement you get one picture. If you compare countries in terms of gap you get another. For example, in overall achievement, the United Kingdom ranked seventh out of thirty-two countries. In comparing the gap between the bottom quarter of student-by-parent-occupation with the top quarter, the UK ranked 26th. In other words, the UK did well on the average because students from high socio-economic backgrounds did so well (OECD, 2000:18).

The reason that this is so important is that societies with sharper socio-economic status gradients or differences have poorer developmental health outcomes (physical and mental health, competence and coping skills) than societies with smaller differences, and are probably less productive in the long run in a knowledge economy (see Keating and Hertzman, 1999).

The societal development argument is difficult and somewhat abstract, but a third ally — in addition to policymakers and educators — not yet mobilized, is the public. By developing better policies and greater capacity at the schoool level, there is great potential for leveraging the public's anxiety into pervasive support for schools. We should not underestimate the depth of moral purpose inherent in the public psyche, especially if this is connected to the improvement of humankind and quality of life through economic and social development.

Michael Barber (2001:1) makes one aspect of the case on behalf of the UK government:

> Across the public services, the government intends to pursue reform with real urgency, not least because it is clear that the public is impatient to see substantial evidence of progress on the ground. In education, this sense of urgency is reinforced not just by the belief that every passing day when a child's education is less than optimal is another day lost, but also the belief that time is running out for public education to prove its worth. The danger is that, as the economies of developed countries grow, more and more people will see private education for their children as a rational lifestyle option ... If this were to occur, they would become correspondingly less willing to pay taxes to fund public education which, over time, would become — in the devastating phrase of the sociologist Richard Titmuss, a generation ago — a poor service for poor people. It is hard to imagine how social cohesion could be achieved and how cascading ever-growing inequality from one generation to another could be prevented under these circumstances. Only if public education delivers — and is seen to deliver — real quality can this unknown prospect be avoided.

I am well aware of power differentials and vested interests in the status quo, but we are talking about new horizons, and if you look closely there is more of a basis for breakthroughs than might be imagined. Bricker (a pollster) and Greenspon (a journalist) have done an excellent job of getting beneath the surface to identify underlying trends and concerns of the general public (in this case, of Canadians). Their analysis is revealing:

> The new mindset on education that emerged over the course of the Nervous Nineties demanded tougher standards, greater discipline, and heightened accountability. Their confidence in education tested, parents felt the need to be able to judge for themselves whether the system was working. But they never abandoned the principles of the public system ... And through the ongoing wars of attrition between teachers and governments, parents at least, never lost sight of the point of the exercise: to prepare their children to prosper in the economy of the future and make a contribution to society overall. The new mindset combined a desire for the system to better reflect the individual needs of children with an understanding that we are all in this together. It believed in choices, but choice in the form of

options within a common public school system — I need help with English, you want computers, she prefers French immersion. Canadians took little interest in the radical choice agenda favored by right-wing reformers fearing such schemes would weaken the public system and produce losers as well as winners. *And as the decade closed, it became evident that the public continued to view schools as critical agents of social cohesion, the common glue that binds society together.* (Bricker and Greenspon, 2001:149, emphasis added)

Sounds like moral purpose to me!

And yes, the public is dissatisfied and anxious about the failure of the school system to keep up, but this means they want to help fix it not abandon it. Bricker and Greenspon argue "that the real public opinion story in education is more about changed expectations than decay in the system. Consumers of education felt the status quo no longer sufficed; they expected far more from the education system than ever before and were unconvinced it could deliver" (p. 156).

Another interesting observation: "despite widespread fears, the connection in Canada has not been severed between the affluent and the public education system. In fact, support for public funding of education generally builds as you move up income and education ladders" (Bricker and Greenspon, 2001:162). In Toronto recently, a group of parents from Rosedale, an affluent area of the city, most of whom send their children to private schools, formed an association to provide political support for greater investment in the public school systems. I would argue not out of guilt, but rather because they were concerned about the government's failure to invest in and strengthen the current system.

While we are at it, let's talk about motives. The highest form of moral purpose is not altruistic martyrdom but a mixture of selfish and unselfish motives. Sober and Wilson (1998) in their study of the evolution of unselfish behavior conclude that it is futile to argue whether people are driven by egoistic (self-centered) or altruistic (unselfish) motives. Effective people are driven by what Sober and Wilson call " 'motivational pluralism' [which] is the view that we have both egoistical and altruistic ultimate desires" (p. 308).

Thus, most of us have mixed motives and that is perfectly fine. It is possible to send your child to a private school, while simultaneously sincerely working to improve the public system; it is morally acceptable to get enormous personal pride out of making a contribution to closing the gap of inequality in your classroom or school or district or state.

What we need, in other words, is to increase the presence of altruistic motives in a manner that does not lessen, indeed may enhance, selfish satisfaction. And yes, there is still a worry, as John Kenneth Galbraith (2002) observed, that those in power often are engaged in "one of man's oldest exercises in moral philosophy; that is the search for a superior moral justification for selfishness."

The point of all this, however, is that no government and no teacher union has appreciated and tapped into the enormous power of the moral purpose concerns and values of the public (not just parents). New horizons will require greater alliance and triangulation of the pluralistic motives of the public, educators and governments.

So, where are we with moral purpose? We may have taken the life out of moral purpose by bandying around all those numbers earlier in this chapter, but the message is crucial and essential if we are to have any chance of accomplishing large-scale, fundamental reform. To recap, the main points are:

- Moral purpose, defined as making a difference in the lives of students, is a critical motivator for addressing the sustained task of complex reform. Passion and higher order purpose are required because the effort needed is gargantuan and must be morally worth doing.
- Moral purpose will not add up if left at the individual level.
- Reducing the gap between high and low performers at all levels (classroom, school, district, state) is the key to system break-throughs.
- Focusing on gap reduction is the moral responsibility of all educators. They must then understand the bigger picture and reach out beyond themselves to work with others.
- Ultimately, a tri-level solution will be necessary (school, district, state) (see Chapters 4–6).
- Reducing the gap in educational attainment is part and parcel of societal development in which greater social cohesion, developmental health and economic performance are at stake.
- Mobilizing the untapped moral purpose of the public in alliance with governments and educators is one of the greatest advances to the cause that we could make.

Four other important conclusions need to be made. First, much of the reducing the gap data referred to in this chapter is based on literacy and numeracy which I have already said represents only first steps on the way to deeper reform. Therefore, additional cognitive and social measures must be sought including indicators that intensive knowledge-centered learning environments are being created on a large scale.

Second, to elevate moral purpose is not to downplay knowledge (Chapter 1). We are talking about major advances in both moral purpose and knowledge, indeed synergies therein. Clearly, for example, strategies for reducing the gap require clever ideas and capacities as well as moral commitments.

Third, the reason that the twin forces of greater knowledge and greater moral commitment beyond individuals are related to sustainability is that they begin to improve the social/moral environment. Those concerned with the depletion of resources in the physical environment were the first to discuss the issue of sustainability. Our concern is the depletion (and enhancement) of resources in the social and moral environment. Only if the social environment improves (other schools around us, for example) will the conditions for continuous improvement be possible. This is another way of altering the context for the better.

Fourth, and most importantly, the informed prescription and accountability schemes of the 1990s and the bloodless test scores at the aggregate level (even those which indicate that the gap of achievement in some jurisdictions is being reduced) have usurped and repressed the development of the very passion and purpose of communities of teachers necessary to take us to new horizons. Peter Block argues that over "how-to" cultures have suppressed deeper deliberations about questions of intention, purpose and responsibility:

> My premise is that this culture, and we as members of it, have yielded too easily to what is doable and practical … In the process we have sacrificed the pursuit of what is in our hearts. We find ourselves giving in to our doubts, and settling for what we know how to do, or can learn to do, instead of pursuing what matters most to us and living with the adventure and anxiety that this requires. (Block, 2002:1)

Freedom, says Block, comes more from commitment than from accomplishment. In the course of pursuing new horizons we need to "create the space for longer discussions about purpose, about what is worth doing" (p. 3). I am not saying that we can afford (or that we will be allowed) to pursue a leisurely dialogue about long-term purpose. The pace and demands of change will still be relentless but it is in our best interest to establish more opportunities for interaction and discussion about the purpose that underlies our strategies as we consider what is being accomplished. These interactions should be designed not to celebrate navel-gazing and other forms of inaction; on the contrary, they are needed precisely in order to unleash the power of educators committed collectively to accomplish reforms never before realized.

But it's a quagmire out there; complexity theory and everyday experience tells us so. We should not, then, be naïve that progress can be blueprinted even with greater knowledge and moral purpose available. The pathways and how-tos are messy and difficult to grasp. We need to step back and consider new insights about the processes of dynamic, complex, non-linear reform.

Chapter 3

New Lessons for Complex Change

*There is a whole host of problems that are not amenable to
authoritative expertise and standard operating procedures.*

Heifetz and Linsky (2002:13)

You cannot get to new horizons without grasping the essence of
complexity theory. The trick is to learn to become a tad more comfort-
able with the awful mystery of complex systems, to do fewer things
to aggravate what is already a centrifugal problem, resist controlling
the uncontrollable, and to learn to use key complexity concepts to
design and guide more powerful learning systems. You need to tweak
and trust the process of change while knowing that it is unpredictable.

We need first to appreciate why we naturally resist complexity
theory: it is too difficult to understand; to the extent we understand
it, we don't want to believe it; it doesn't seem to be very usable, and
so on. Let's start with the mystery and then try to extract some
practicality.

Marion (1999:xii) expresses it this way:

> Chaos theory, or rather that branch of chaos theory that we will
> identify as complexity theory, responds that order emerges naturally
> because of unpredictable interaction — interaction is the vehicle by
> which this occurs and unpredictability is the stimulus that promotes
> novelty ... The argument proposed in this book is that intersecting
> entities — atoms, molecules, people, organizations — tend (a) to
> correlate with one another because of their interaction, and (b) to
> catalyze aggregation. Correlation is what happens when two or more
> people exert interactive influence over one another ... Auto-catalysis
> — the second point — begins when the behavior of one system
> stimulates certain behaviors in another system that in turn stimulates
> another and another; eventually the chain of stimulation returns to
> motivate, or catalyze, the original system and the cycle is reinforced.
> Order, then, emerges not because someone or something expends

energy to create it; rather order emerges from the natural, and free, consequences of interaction.

No politician is going to get elected, or no candidate appointed to a leadership position on a platform of correlation, auto-catalysis, and trust-me-order-will-come. But there is some, at least intuitive hope, even at the theoretical level.

> Chaotic order per se is actually too violent, too changing to describe much that goes on among living beings. Complexity theorists, who are conceptually related to chaos theorists, argue that life tunes chaos's intensity down a bit to a transition between chaos and predictable stability called the edge of chaos. Dynamics in this band are still chaotic but they also possess characteristics of order. Full-blown chaotic systems have little memory; living systems must be able to map their pasts. Chaotic systems flit a bit too readily from novelty to novelty; living systems need to consolidate gains. Predictable, stable systems, by contrast, possess none of the panache needed to create new order or even to respond adaptively to creature environments. Complex systems lie between these poles, at the edge of chaos; and they have both panache and stability sufficient to serve life. (Marion, 1999:xiv)

My argument, in effect, is that Phase I solutions discussed in Chapter 1, namely, informed prescription, necessarily impose order on an unproductive chaotic system, but that Phase II solutions, informed professional and public judgment, will require the creative thinking of complexity theory. Chaos, uninformed, is bad; informed order is better; complexity is best.

In this chapter I am going to push the practical (but still complex) elements of complexity theory in a way that policymakers and practitioners can find usable. As a segue to the usable, we can remind ourselves of some of the core concepts of complexity theory:

- *Non-linearity*: don't expect reforms to unfold as intended
- *Unpredictability*: surprises will happen as a result of dynamically complex interactive forces
- *Interaction or correlation*: a key element of moving towards order
- *Auto-catalysis*: occurs when systems interact and influence each other toward new patterns
- *The edge of chaos*: (could just as easily be called the edge of order) when systems avoid too little and too much order

- *Social attractors*: (originally strange attractors in chaos theory) compelling social motivators — can extract periodic patterns of order (consolidate gains) as complex system dynamics unfold
- *Butterfly effects*: (when small numbers of key forces coalesce) — can have disproportionately huge effects
- *A complex adaptive system* — consists of high degrees of internal interaction, and interaction externally (with other systems) in a way that constitutes continuous learning.

Remember that the eventual solution for Phase II educational reform is that the vast majority of people in the system must end up "owning the problem" and be the agents of its solution (Heifetz and Linsky, 2002). This is absolutely not to say that the problem should be handed over to people; we need instead to create the conditions and processes that will enhance the likelihood that we move down the path of increasingly greater ownership and commitment.

In common sense terms:

- Start with the notion of moral purpose, key problems, desirable directions, but don't lock in.
- Create communities of interaction around these ideas.
- Ensure that quality information infuses interaction and related deliberations.
- Look for and extract promising patterns, i.e., consolidate gains and build on them.

We are now in a position to provide more helpful ideas for design and action. In each of the previous two books in the *Change Forces* trilogy, I have formulated eight guidelines for dealing with change forces in complex times (Fullan, 1993, 1999). The new eight guidelines are deeply compatible with the theories just presented. They have the added virtue of being resonant with current multi-year initiatives in which we are involved across countries.

Figure 3.1 contains the eight lessons for *Change Forces With a Vengeance*. They are congruent with the previous two sets, but they have three additional distinguishing characteristics: (1) they are more amenable to action, design and strategizing; (2) they assume large-scale reform is the goal; (3) they pursue the ultimate question of sustainability. All eight lessons feed on each other. No one lesson can be treated in isolation. They can put us more in the driver's seat, albeit in a bus that is sometimes out of control.

Lesson 1:   Give up the idea that the pace of change will slow down.

Lesson 2:   Coherence making is a never-ending proposition and is everyone's responsibility.

Lesson 3:   Changing context is the focus.

Lesson 4:   Premature clarity is a dangerous thing.

Lesson 5:   The public's thirst for transparency is irreversible.

Lesson 6:   You can't get large-scale reform through bottom-up strategies — but beware of the trap.

Lesson 7:   Mobilize the social attractors — moral purpose, quality relationships, quality knowledge.

Lesson 8:   Charismatic leadership is negatively associated with sustainability.

Figure 3.1 Complex change lessons

Lesson 1: Give up the idea that the pace of change will slow down

You don't have to go very far into complexity theory to realize that it is a mug's game to hope for the speed of change to slow down. James Glieck, the author of *Chaos*, wrote a recent book which he entitled *Faster* (the subtitle was *The Acceleration of Just About Everything*) (Gleick, 1999). It would be naïve to hope that the overall pace of change will noticeably decrease. It would be a sure-fire recipe for unsustainability to think "if only we can get through the next three years with this particular reform, we will be okay." Frustration and burnout are the most likely outcomes of this mindset.

There are alternatives to being steamrolled by change and many of the ideas in the other lessons, and in the other chapters, constitute a set of capacities for dealing with rampant change. None of them objectively slow down change. All of them increase our capacity to cope with the messiness of complexity, by achieving greater coherence and focus.

We can begin by not trying to resist the irresistible, which is relentless change. Paul Baker, Professor Emeritus at Illinois State University, spent his entire career studying the experiences of teachers and administrators with educational reform in Illinois, only to conclude:

> Planned change for [educators] is not the cumulative development of a comprehensive strategy. Rather, it is "one damned thing after another." (Baker *et al.*, 1991:13)

A good starting point is to develop a more relaxed attitude toward uncertainty; to not have expectations of the system that it is incapable of meeting, and then to work on those more subtle more powerful change forces that can bring greater results over time. As Saul (1997:222) puts it: "The ability to assume complexity is a great strength. You could call it the ability to deal with reality."

Soon we begin to realize that it is not the pace of change that is the culprit, it is the piecemealness and fragmentation that wears us down. You can do something about this, but it requires continuous work and more patience because it is never fully solvable. Hence, lesson two, a positive step for coping with the pace of reform.

Lesson 2: Coherence making is a never-ending proposition and is everyone's responsibility

Accept rapid pace, and work on coherence making. When Fred Newmann and his colleagues studied school capacity (more about this in Chapter 4) their model assumed that "policies and programs external to schools (at the district or state levels) could enhance capacity at the school level" (Newmann *et al.*, 2000). Unfortunately, they did not come across any strong example of this happening. This is another way of saying that the wider infrastructure is *theoretically* important as a coherence maker but empirically there do not yet seem to be many examples of it. If anything, the larger system has contributed to greater overload, fragmentation and episodic initiatives that come and go in disjointed ways — what Tom Hatch (2000) called the problem of multiple innovations constantly colliding.

One of the reasons for the success of the National Literacy and Numeracy Strategy in England (Chapter 1) is that policymakers deliberately worked on policy alignment by developing and coordinating strategies for standards, assessment, curriculum and instruction, professional development, leadership development, and so on. As we saw in Chapter 1, Connecticut was similarly successful in improving the teaching profession through a coherent set of policy initiatives that integrated new standards for teachers, teacher preparation, induction, continuous professional development, and various related leadership roles to support and assess these interrelated reforms.

By contrast, California had limited success in its major mathematics reform because it did not focus on coordinating the three major policy levers of assessment, curriculum, and teacher learning. This is not just a matter of aligning policies on paper or in the minds of policymakers. This kind of "contrived coherence" remains at the state level and represents no experienced coherence at the local level. Cohen and Hill (2001:186) refer to this superficial coherence as "a crippling problem; for coherence at the level of state guidelines is only the first of many steps that could lead to coherence among the instruments and agents of instruction." They continue:

> The evidence from this study ... strongly suggests that coherence in instructional policy is unlikely to pay off handsomely for teaching and learning unless it is manifest both in the materials of instruction — especially assessment and curriculum — and in the curriculum for professionals' learning. (p. 186)

There are no short cuts to coherence. This is one reason why externally developed whole school reform models are bound to fail. The models, for example, sponsored by the New American Schools corporation (NAS), such as "Success for All," have the apparent virtue of being comprehensive and internally aligned. Even in places like Memphis in which there was strong system support these models have a relatively short shelf-life (Franceschini, 2002).

Why? Because no matter how you dice it, they are imported coherence. I am not against using the models provided they are seen as a means to help people figure out their own coherence (although they are actually unlikely to work that way). People should be seeking ideas that help them develop their own thinking rather than "programs." The latter, at best, is a means to an end. In Chapter 5 we will see that NAS (2002) is in the midst of changing its strategy to focus on system reform precisely because of the limitation of depending on external models.

Another caution: Recall that operating on the edge of chaos means also resisting the temptation to impose too much order. All this does is give the appearance of control. Policymakers, especially if they are to go to Phase II transformation, will have to design policy levers which give them a little less control than they would like (they never had it anyway) in exchange for the potential of higher yield innovation and commitment on the ground.

The lesson here for policymakers is not to attempt to achieve perfect coherence, but rather (a) stop compounding the problem by adding even greater incoherence through piecemeal reforms, and (b) don't think you can achieve coherence through policy alignment at the top — it is only the start.

Even more interesting, I think, is the realization from complexity theory that since patterns of order require local interaction — patterns of order achieved in the context of overall complexity in the larger environment — *it is equally critical for individuals, small groups, organizations to figure out and link to the bigger picture.* One of the characteristics that distinguish particularly effective leaders in organizations is their capacity to grasp and relate to the big picture (see Chapter 7).

What I am saying is crucial for large-scale reform and sustainability. Both policymakers and local practitioners have *equal* responsibility to connect the dots. We are talking about big picture dot-connection of the kind that integrates new horizons and moral purpose. The goal is to create new policies, strategies and mechanisms that enable people to enlarge their own worlds in order to provide greater ideas and place the meaning of their work in a much larger perspective. When people do this they have a chance of changing the very context that historically constrains them.

Lesson 3: Changing context is the focus

The context is usually seen as a set of *conditions* under which we operate. It is assumed that these circumstances contain variables we can't control. Well, they may be hard to alter but transformative change by definition means changing the context. Individual backgrounds can't be fixed because they are in the past; contexts can be because they are now.

It turns out that there may be more hope and more reason for working on contextual change than we might have thought. In *The Tipping Point*, Malcolm Gladwell (2000), identifies the "power of context" as one of three agents of change (the other two we will take up in Lesson 7 — the "law of the few" and the "stickiness factor." The power of context says that "people are a lot more sensitive to their environment than they may seem" (Gladwell, 2000:29). Thus, to change immediate context, even in small ways can result in new behaviors — in short order.

Gladwell uses the so-called "broken windows" theory to introduce the point that context is more powerful than individual predispositions:

> Broken Windows was the brainchild of the criminologists, James Q. Wilson and George Kelling. Wilson and Kelling argued that crime is the inevitable result of disorder. If a window is broken and left unrepaired, people walking by will conclude that no one cares and no one is in charge. Soon more windows will be broken, and the sense of anarchy will spread from the building to the street on which it faces, sending a signal that anything goes. In a city, relatively

minor problems like graffiti, public disorder, and aggressive panhandling ... are all the equivalent of broken windows, invitations to more serious crimes. (p. 141)

New York City, of course, applied the broken windows theory in the late 1980s and 1990s to crack down on minor crimes which created a new context that contributed to what turned out to be a dramatic decrease in violent crimes. Says Gladwell, "Broken Windows theory and the Power of Context are one and the same" (p. 146).

We are talking about the edge of chaos, so that imposing too much control can backfire (or in our previous reference to David Hargreaves' policy levers, a lever which works for one phase of a change process can mistakenly be overused to attempt deeper changes for which it is not capable).

Nonetheless, there is a critical generalizable message for complexity theory and our interest in contextual transformation:

When it comes to interpreting other people's behavior, human beings invariably make the mistake of overestimating the importance of fundamental character traits and underestimating the importance of the situation and context. We will always reach for a "dispositional" explanation for events as opposed to a contextual explanation. (Gladwell, 2000:160)

Gladwell reports a number of experiments when context carried the day over individual predisposition. Apropos of our earlier discussion of the PISA study, Gladwell makes the same point: "studies of juvenile delinquency and high school drop-out rates ... demonstrate that a child is better off in a good neighborhood and a troubled family than he or she is in a troubled neighborhood and a good family" (pp 167–8). And, "it is possible to be a better person on a clean street or in a clean subway than in one littered with trash and graffiti."

The message for us is don't treat the context as a given. Change it, even in small ways, to get new results. If you want more sharing of knowledge, name it as a value, create mechanisms that cause it to happen, and have low tolerance for people who don't do it (see Fullan, 2001b, Chapter 5). When you get new behaviors, reinforce them, consolidate gains and go even further.

In short, the power of context is historically seen as a forceful constraint. In the new age the power of new contexts is treated deliberately as a necessary agent of change. Once people realize the change potential of context, and begin to direct their efforts at changing it, the breakthroughs can be amazing. Context is one of those very high yield policy levers that David Hargreaves (2002) talks about. Finally, as before, altering context is not up to others; all of us can, to a certain extent, change the immediate context around us — and this starts us down the pathway of transformation.

Lesson 4: Premature clarity is a dangerous thing

When you are facing a complex problem with a sense of urgency there is nothing more seductive than an off the shelf solution, the clarity of charisma or anything that provides the comfort of a clear direction. Resist it. This seduction is what prompted Peter Drucker, Professor Emeritus of Business, who reputedly observed that "people refer to gurus because they don't know how to spell charlatan."

Heifetz and Linsky (2002) make the distinction between technical change and adaptive change. We tend to know the answers to the former but not the latter. Technical change — hard enough — is improving literacy and numeracy. Adaptive change is transformation of the system:

> Every day, people have problems for which they do, in fact, have the necessary know-how and procedures. We call these technical problems. But there is a whole host of problems that are not amenable to authoritative expertise or standard operating procedures. They cannot be solved by someone who provides the answers from on high. We call these adaptive challenges because they require experiments, new discoveries, and adjustments from numerous places in the organization or community. Without learning new ways — changing attitudes, values, and behaviors — people cannot make the adaptive leap necessary to thrive in new environments. The *sustainability* of change depends on having the people with the problem internalize the change itself. (Heifetz and Linsky, 2002: 13, emphasis added)

In other words, for complex adaptive problems, the main role of policymakers is not so much to implement clarity as it is to help people discover it. There are two major reasons why we must resist premature clarity. First, the solutions to fundamental transformation of educational systems resulting in sustainable capacities have never yet been achieved, and therefore are not knowable in advance. Second, and more fundamental, no solution for sustainability leaves out people struggling through the anxieties of complex problem solving toward shared solutions:

The more challenging the problem, the more people who will bear the consequences of its solution must take responsibility for working on it. (Heifetz and Linsky, 2002:4)

In transformational change, we are dealing with more than technical matters: "people's hearts and minds need to change, and not just their preferences or routine behaviors" (Heifetz and Linsky, 2002:60). We need to combine moral purpose, engagement with others and the ideas and resources that have some hope of getting us there. Heifetz and Linsky (2002:94) observe, "People are willing to make sacrifices if they see the reason why ... people need to know the stakes are worth it."

Premature and false clarity, if convincingly presented, are dangerous precisely because they can capture people's hearts and minds — thereby leading them down ill-conceived pathways. Clarity generated through interaction, problem solving, and communities of practice, delays premature closure enough so that the checks and balances of complexity theory serve to scrutinize ideas. People in learning communities learn "to talk back," and to be skeptical about imposed ideas. They are in a better position to question external solutions. But we don't want people to turn inward, which is groupthink. False clarity, external or internal, is equally dangerous. This is why the public's thirst for transparency is a good thing.

Lesson 5: The public's thirst for transparency is irreversible (and on balance this is a good thing)

The quest for clear evidence of student learning is not without its problems, but let's be clear that it is here to stay. We can no longer credibly argue against it; we need instead to become more sophisticated about data. Bricker and Greenspon (2001:165) state it bluntly:

> ... one of the most striking findings in our research is the overwhelming level of support for student and teacher testing. The time is well past when parents accepted as an article of faith that their children were on the receiving end of a good education and that teachers and schools were equipping them for the challenges of the future. The decline of public trust and the concurrent drift of schools from social to economic institutions [you need a good education to survive in the knowledge economy] has ushered in an evidence-based show-me age. Parents are insisting upon independent, objective, and measurable information. Without transparency, the search for certainty is futile.

Michael Barber, the head of the policy delivery unit in Prime Minister Tony Blair's office in the U.K. makes a similar point:

> In my view, we will not see a reverse of the 10–15 years of travel towards openness in relation to performance — on the contrary, I think it will intensify. We can expect individual teacher data to become much more widely available. In the National Health Service data by consultant will become available soon ... Transparency about everything will be a key theme in the next 20 years (look at the corporate debate post-Enron). Informed professionals will find themselves individually as well as collectively accountable. (personal communication, May 27, 2002)

This is why we include assessment literacy (not literacy assessment) in our training with school and district teams. Assessment literacy is a high yield strategy that increases the collective capacity of educators:

- To gather/access student performance data
- To critically analyze (disaggregate, interpret) such data
- To develop action plans for improvement
- To discuss and debate the meaning of data in public fora.

The first three are critical for internal improvement, the fourth for external accountability. In effect, teachers and administrators must be able to enter the debate concerning the uses and abuses of assessment data, and not be cowed by it, but rather to hold their own and indeed be influential in educating parents, the public, the media and policymakers. I am very aware that just because you are paranoid doesn't mean that someone is *not* out to get you, but the fact is that once complexity theory gets hold of transparency, you can run but you can't hide. In this era of "leave no child untested," it is crucial for educators to become assessment literate.

The best defense against the abuse of information is an informed offense. Teachers are "target-tired" in England and other places. And you don't have to have targets to have transparency. Wales has the latter but not the former, although my guess is that targets could become a lot less threatening if educators were assessment literate. Assessment literacy, incidentally, means critiquing the inadequacy of current assessment schemes and widening the range of indicators of student performance.

Anyway, who could blame the public for becoming suspicious? One of the fallouts of the accountability press of the 1980s was a growing mistrust on the part of the public. As specific criticisms mounted against the public school systems (I am not saying that they were accurate in every case), educators responded vaguely and defensively: you can't measure what's really important; each school is unique and comparing them is misleading; we are teaching the whole child, etc. Generalized responses to specific criticisms on a vital matter breeds skepticism. What if teachers couldn't explain themselves in convincing terms because many of them really didn't know what they were doing? (This is why collective informed professional judgment is such a powerful strategy — people get to know what they are doing and can explain it).

The same is true for teacher assessment. As a blunt instrument it can do more harm than good. But if part of a comprehensive set of capacity-building policies to uplift the profession, as is the case in Connecticut, it becomes a different story (Wilson *et al.*, 2001).

Complexity theory basically tells us to take the risk of developing open, interactive, quality information systems, guided by moral purpose, and then look for promising patterns to reinforce and build on. Parents and the public want to see schools improved. Trust that the public is capable of developing informed judgment, but it won't happen without transparency and it doesn't always have to be based on narrow measurement. As trust develops the public is capable of understanding qualitative arguments. In any case, informed public judgment is key to large-scale, sustainable reform because that is where the ultimate source of investment and support lies.

As Bricker and Greenspon (2001:163) observe, the Canadian public seems to be talking to teachers and government alike:

> Yes, we're concerned about the educational system. We want to be assured it's keeping pace with the new challenges being thrown its way. But don't use this as an excuse to pursue ideological or fiscal agendas. We believe in our public school system. We want it strengthened, not gutted. And we want to be able to sleep comfortably, knowing it's working for our kids.

Public support is a terrible thing to squander if you are interested in transformational reform.

Lesson 6: You can't get large-scale reform through bottom-up strategies — but beware of the trap

Here is the paradox. You need ownership for fundamental change, but you can't get it on a large-scale by relying on bottom-up strategies. If you base a strategy on investing only in local development, what happens is: (a) not much of the bottom moves, or (b) some of it moves in the wrong way, or (c) some of it moves productively, but the good ideas don't get around, nor do they persist for very long. This is another way of saying that "the top" matters — the larger infrastructure really is crucial for system change. Let us also remember that mandated change has a very poor track record, and even if England's literacy and numeracy strategy has been successful it is a rare exception.

All of our examples of Phase I (literacy and numeracy improvements) success on a large-scale had a strong degree of front-end, assertive top-down leadership. This is true for England, and for school district successes (see Chapter 5). In a sense, you can get away with top-down leadership under two conditions: (1) if it turns out you had a good idea (informed prescription) and (2) if you invest in capacity-building (and empowerment) from day one. But this still only brings us large-scale, first-steps (not deep or sustainable reform).

The trap is that as policymakers get results from assertive strategies they are inclined to intensify the strategies that got them to the present. This is a classic edge of chaos problem. Chaos or drift is bad, corrective order is good, but pushing the limits of order backfires. We will discuss San Diego as an interesting case in Chapter 5. Strategies based on top-down initiative and bottom-up capacity-building which were successful in School District #2 in New York City were introduced with fierce intensity and a great sense of urgency in San Diego. Leaders facing systems of drift will argue that the system needed a rough wakeup call, and they may be right. But once you get people awake, you may have to do something different sooner rather than later. But it is incredibly difficult for anyone, let alone those who have been successful with a certain strategy, to figure out the balance between chaos and order. Too much chaos brings us back to where we started. Too much order leads to fear, resistance or perhaps even worse, passive dependency.

The good news is that once you start down the path of large-scale reform you inevitably discover that you are talking about *changing the system* if you want to go the distance. You become more open to considering alternatives, you become convinced that ownership and creativity at all levels are essential. You become, in short, more intrigued by the lessons of complexity theory because they make intuitive sense. You become more open to new policy levers, based on such conceptions.

I cannot claim that we know exactly how to accomplish sustainability or system transformation, because no one has ever done it before.

But I can say that there is enough theoretical argument and instances of strategic evidence to build on. Anyone who has worked on large-scale reform will find these conceptions and evidence convincing enough to want to work on them. Thus, we need a new generation of policy initiatives and grand experiments (inquiry-based with corrective mechanisms as we go), which are designed to produce much greater yields than even our best current large-scale reform efforts. Nothing could be more powerful in the service of this quest than strategies that mobilize the social attractors.

Lessons 7: Mobilize the social attractors — moral purpose, quality relationships, quality knowledge

We need to name the problem more clearly. It is not just a matter of ownership. We are asking people to enter new terrain where they have never gone before. Heifetz and Linsky (2002:30) describe it this way:

> Adaptive change stimulates resistance because it challenges people's habits, beliefs, and values. It asks them to take a loss, experience uncertainty, and even express disloyalty to people and cultures. Because adaptive change forces people to question and perhaps redefine aspects of their identity, it also challenges their sense of competence. Loss, disloyalty, and feeling incompetent: That's a lot to ask. No wonder people resist.

Stated differently, when we are trying something radically new the losses are immediate and practical while the potential gains are longer term and theoretical. Since it *is* a lot to ask, we need powerful social attractors. One set, of course, is moral purpose of the kind described in Chapter 2. If people believe they are doing something worthwhile of a higher order they may be willing to put in the extra sacrifices and effort. It is also a matter of trust. It is not just the *actions* of governments that count but also the perceived integrity and motivation. This applies to both the public and the teaching profession. Speaking about Ontario, Bricker and Greenspon (2001:161) say:

> While certain aspects of the reforms — accountability and discipline, in particular — have proven popular, the government has never overcome the suspicion that its actions have been motivated by ideology and money rather than what's best for kids.

Similarly, teachers will accept more demands of accountability from governments whose motives they trust, that is, from governments that they perceive are genuinely interested in improvement — in a word from governments who operate with moral as well as political purpose.

Moral purpose is not enough. We also need the enormous power of people working together. We need to minimize the severe debilitating negativity of people in constant conflict; and avoid even the lost opportunities of people being too nice to each other, or otherwise avoiding confronting problems.

If we are going to develop quality relationships of the order required for transformational change we will need to redefine our approach to resistance so that we draw on the valid critiques and energy of those skeptical of given new directions. In speaking of leadership, Heifetz and Linsky (2002:89) elaborate:

> People who oppose what you are trying to accomplish are usually those with the most to lose by your success. In contrast, your allies have the least to lose. For opponents to turn around will cost them dearly in terms of disloyalty to their own roots and constituency; for your allies to come along may cost nothing. For that reason, your opponents deserve more of your attention, as a matter of compassion, as well as a tactic of strategy and survival.

We also know that quality relationships, once they do develop inspire great loyalty. Studies of courageous actions in war indicate that it is not so much moral purpose that lies behind putting your life on the line (although that can be part of it) but the more tangible presence of loyalty to your buddies. Quality relationships in other words, are even more powerful than moral purpose, which is another way of expressing the power of context.

In the absence of quality relationships every solution costs money. Without trust, people, at best, will only do things you pay them for; with trust, people will double your investment and go the extra mile. To say the obvious, we need resources beyond money to achieve transformation.

The third set of social attractors is quality ideas: knowledge building, knowledge sharing and constantly converting information into purposeful knowledge use. Content does matter, since there is no point having moral purpose and great relationships without them being fueled by great ideas.

Recall Gladwell's *Tipping Point*. More generally, says, Gladwell (2000:258):

> What most underlies successful epidemics, in the end, is a bedrock belief that change is possible, that people can radically transform their behavior or beliefs in the face of the right kind of impetus.

The right kind of impetus, or "tipping point" may not be as massive as we think; powerful, and the right kind yes, but not necessarily huge. *Tipping Point* is complexity theory — little causes can have big effects. These little causes from Gladwell are three: the power of context, the law of few (a small but critical mass of key change agents), and the stickiness factor (a message or idea that is memorable or sticks in your head).

My three are: the social attractors of moral purpose, quality relationships and quality ideas. Moral purpose and quality ideas need to have sticky qualities (memorable inspiration and ideas that move us to action); new relationships need the law of the few to help kick start the process in order to create new role models and contexts. These new contexts need not be dramatically different to stimulate new behaviors.

Social attractors have substance. They are the draws that cause new order to arise from disorder. Moral purpose gives people a glimpse of the future:

> ... the positive vision that makes the current angst worthwhile ... by making the vision more tangible, reminding people of the values they are fighting for, and showing them how the future might look. By answering, in every possible way, the "why" question, you increase people's willingness to endure the hardships that come with the journey to a better place. (Heifetz and Linsky, 2002:120–1)

Even if the future isn't clear, strong moral purpose helps "to embody hope rather than fear" (Heifetz and Linsky, 2002:122).

Equally powerful, and in some ways more so is to strengthen peer commitments ("knowing people well enough so what they think of you matters" in the words of Gladwell, 2000:186). Quality relationships change contexts in ways that cause people to behave differently.

Without quality ideas, we would be merely reinforcing each other's good intentions with nothing to show for it. Content as well as context matters.

Finally, for education, social attractors are critical because of the social cohesion role of the public education system. Patterns of concentrated efforts among educators are needed to solve problems, close learning gaps among groups, and build joint commitment for sustained action. In short, we must design education systems which strengthen the power of attractors.

Lesson 8: Charismatic leadership is negatively associated with sustainability

Leadership is crucial to fostering the conditions that are necessary to create new tipping points, but once again, complexity theory sets a trap. There are no shortcuts, for example, by hiring especially visionary leaders. The evidence is mounting that charismatic or savior-type leaders are dangerous to the long-term health of organizations. Collins (2001) analyzed in detail 11 companies that experienced sustained economic performance over a minimum of 15 years, and compared them to other companies that had short-term growth. He makes the same distinction I make in Chapter 1 between Phase I and Phase II new horizons. Collins (2001:20) distinguishes between the Level 4 effective leader who "catalyzes commitment to and vigorous pursuit of a clear and compelling vision, stimulating higher performance standards" and the Level 5 effective leader who "builds enduring greatness" in the organization.

Charismatic leaders can achieve short-term increases in student achievement results or short-term profits in business, but it turns out that this is at the *expense* of longer-term development. Collins (2001:21) found that charismatic leaders were negatively associated with sustainable performance (over 15 years or more). The 11 leaders who helped build enduring greatness were not high profile flashy performers but rather "individuals who blend extreme personal humility with intense professional will." They are strong, but strong in the right ways.

Recent colossal collapses of apparently invincibly successful businesses painfully teach the same lesson. Based on research on chief executive officer successions at 850 companies, Khurana (2002) entitled his book, *Searching for a Corporate Savior: The Irrational Quest for Charismatic CEOs*. In a summary article he writes:

> In recent years, corporations seeking to entice investors began making "charisma" an important qualification for the position of chief executive officer. Today, with each new revelation of a CEO's grandiose promises falling flat — or of actual corporate wrong doing — the folly of relying on this leadership model is becoming clearer. Since Enron's demise last September and the most recent revelations of CEOs expropriating billions of dollars from shareholders at Tyco,

> Adelphia and WorldCom, a shadow has been cast not just on corporations in general, but on CEOs in particular. (*Toronto Globe & Mail*, Wednesday, July 3, 2002, A11)

Violating almost every principle of complexity theory visionary CEOs project (false) optimism, inspire employees to take unwarranted risks, squelch criticism, and generally fail to develop intelligence and leadership across the organization. Says Khurana:

> Charismatic authority, by its very nature discourages criticism. Visionary leaders generally do not respond well to questions or complaints. However, without being able to hear any critical questioning voices, the charismatic leader in a large complex organization has no way of knowing whether he or she is being effective — let alone whether the pursuit of grandiose visions has led across legal or ethical boundaries that should not be crossed … faith in the vision of charismatic leaders is a poor organizing principle for contemporary firms which increasingly depend on the sharing of intelligence and the dispersal of decision-making authority across all levels of the organization. (*Toronto Globe & Mail*, July 3, 2002)

Charismatic leaders disdain the lessons contained in this chapter. They don't mind fast-paced change; they are pleased to provide coherence, however misleading; they change the context in superficial ways; they are masters of premature clarity; they hate transparency because it cramps their style; they know nothing — or care nothing about the trap of top-down reform; and the only attractor they believe in is themselves.

We need instead, leaders at many levels. Part and parcel of sustainability in organizations is the way in which they constantly spawn leadership and commitment in all quarters by fostering the flourishing of the intelligence, purpose and passion of all members of the organization.

The eight lessons in this chapter obviously do not provide a blueprint for the future. Greatness can never be so formulated. Taken together they do complexity proud, because they operate to provide checks and balances, and more importantly the power of forward movement toward deeper and more sustainable reform. They help you survive as well as periodically thrive on the edge of chaos.

Chapter 4

Tri-Level Reform: The School

Companies at the forefront of the knowledge economy are succeeding on the basis of communities of practice, whatever they call them.

Wenger, McDermott and Snyder, 2002:3

It is interesting to realize that relationships have more power and passion than moral purpose. The goal, of course, is to get them to team up because we have a very long way to go in educational reform. A superficial application of complexity theory will not do the job. The principles of this theory have very deep meaning. As Marion (1999:212) says about the butterfly effect (small happenings can generate large consequences):

> If the flapping of a butterfly's wings in Texas can dramatically change weather patterns in Chicago, then the flapping of one's mouth or seemingly innocuous decisions, or random behaviors, can dramatically affect an organization's future... Indeed.

It is not any old butterfly's action that counts but particular ones, and they have to occur in interaction with certain factors and conditions.

In this chapter I will establish the tri-level argument, indicate the nature and depth of the educational change we are talking about at the school level, and then hammer home the point with complexity theory.

The tri-level argument

The tri-level argument is that educational transformation will require changes (new capacities) within each of three levels and across their relationships. The levels are: the school (this chapter), the district (Chapter 5), and the state (Chapter 6).

As we will soon see, we need dramatically more intensive interaction within schools, across schools within districts, across districts, and between districts and the state (we could, of course, add a fourth level — global/cross-nation interaction, but that is for another time).

What this amounts to is enacting the complexity theory principles of correlation and auto-catalysis we discussed in the previous chapter. Correlation is what happens when individuals increase their interaction and exert greater influence over one another creating new convergent patterns; auto-catalysis is when the behavior of one system stimulates certain behaviors in another system that, in turn, stimulates another and so on, eventually returning to motivate the original system thereby reinforcing a cycle of development and learning.

This means that if we can get the right kind of intensive interaction going, say among teachers within a school, we will get new correlations, i.e., new behaviors. In effect, the result will be a reduction in the variations of teaching across classrooms. Similarly, if a school interacts on some ongoing basis with other schools or schools with a district, or districts with states, these systems will affect each other. I made the case in Chapters 1 and 2 that interaction is a necessary condition for reform and that the content of the interaction must be continually subjected to the discipline of new ideas and moral purpose.

The tri-level case is that you cannot get transformation by going it alone. We also do not want to have to wait for other levels to get their acts together. More insightfully, we have to help other levels get started. In so doing, auto-catalysis causes us to change as we work with others who are changing. In short, each level has two responsibilities — work hard at increasing interaction within your level; work hard at increasing exchanges across levels. The former will be more intensive than the latter, but both are ongoing and influence each other. Dramatic increases in these types of interaction are required for transformation. Right now, schools and schools systems are decidedly not like this — structurally, normatively, culturally.

How deep is your change?

Examples of success so far are not very deep. The advances in literacy and numeracy in School District #2 in New York, and in the English system are impressive, but relatively superficial. The good work of Fred Newmann and his colleagues focusing on school capacity — increases in teacher knowledge, professional community, program coherence, technical resources, and principal leadership — is also valuable but only a start (Newmann *et al.*, 2000). And these are among the best examples, representing at most ten percent of schools and districts.

Richard Elmore (2002a:22) makes the case:

> People who work in schools do not pay attention to the connections
> between how they organize and manage themselves and how they
> take care of their own and their student's learning.

Far from laying blame on individual teachers, Elmore argues (and
this is the point of this book) that the system has not nearly tried to
establish the conditions for this to happen. In another paper Elmore
(2003) takes on performance based accountability systems and what
he calls "stakes" (measuring performance coupled with rewards and
sanctions). Not that he is against them, but rather that currently they
lack all the depth required to be successful. Elmore acknowledges
that the intent of the policies is honorable, namely, that performance
based accountability is necessary for large-scale improvements in
student learning, school quality and addressing the achievement gap.
He goes on to state:

> State policies require proficiency levels for grade promotion and
> graduation for students … without any empirical evidence or any
> defensible theory about how much it is feasible to expect students
> to learn over a given period of time, or what types of instruction
> have to be in place in order for students to meet expected rates of
> improvement. (Elmore, 2003:3)

Closer to our point:

> Can people in schools be held accountable for their effects on student
> learning if they haven't been provided the opportunity to acquire
> the new knowledge and skill necessary to produce the performance
> that is expected of them? (p. 7)

Incidentally, this includes knowledge and skill which remain to be
developed as we don't actually know how to go deeper in many
cases, and hence we need learning systems that will work on problems
and produce new discoveries.

The purpose of stakes, or any incentive designed to affect academic
performance, is "to mobilize commitment, energy, and knowledge
around the students and teachers mutual engagement in the content"
(p. 12).

This, says Elmore, takes us to the problem of organizations:

... ineffective teachers, can, other things being equal, easily pass their failures onto others, and the success of teachers and students at Time 2 is heavily mediated by the success of the same students with other teachers in Time 1. It is impossible, in other words, to solve the problem of increasing the performance of teachers and students in one classroom without also solving that problem in schools and school systems. (p. 16)

Elmore then concludes:

It is absolutely essential to understand that when policies lay down stakes on incoherent organizations, *the stakes themselves do not cause the organization to become more coherent and effective.* The stakes are mediated and refracted by the organizations on which they fall. Stakes, if they work at all, do so by mobilizing resources, capacities, knowledge, and competencies that by definition *are not present in the organizations and individuals* whom they are intended to affect. If the schools have these assets in advance of the stakes, they would presumably not need the stakes to mobilize them. (p. 18, emphasis in original)

Elmore's point is that not only do you need incentives and accountability mechanisms, but you also need theories of action and strategies that are effective at developing the *capacities* required to respond to the incentives and demands of accountability. Elsewhere, Elmore (2002b) makes a powerful case for "reciprocal accountability" in which the system invests in capacity development in return for more accountable performance.

Similar points have been made by Cohen and Hill (2001) in their detailed study of mathematics reform in California, which we discussed in Chapter 1. Essentially, they argue (a) that the depth of pedagogical reform involved is considerable, and (b) that 90 percent of teachers, or more, do not have the intensive, aligned learning opportunities which would be necessary to engage them in the reform at a substantial level. "Design of learning environments" (Bransford *et al.*, 1999) carries the same message. Learner-centered/knowledge-centered/assessment-centered systems of learning for all are highly sophisticated in-depth pedagogical reforms which require much greater individual and collective capacity than now exists in school systems.

We see the dilemma. We need schools with these powerful learning capacities; this requires the full engagement of and commitment of students and teachers; we need it on a large scale; we don't now have it. In other words, how do you get deep new commitments and capacities across thousands of units in a very large complex system? We are getting ahead of ourselves, but the general answer is through tri-level developments, which means we have a hell of a lot of work to do.

What can individual teachers and schools do? They can understand the agenda; start working together, especially if led by supportive principals and teacher leaders; they can seek external linkages that have capacity-building resources. Leaders, especially, can do a great deal to help reculture schools (see Chapter 7 and Fullan, 2001, Fullan, in press). There are limits to what can be done by individuals (and indeed this is the point of the tri-level solution), but inaction is not one of the options because systems won't change that way.

I have not said anything about parents and the community. There are a number of concomitant developments which are necessary but outside the focus of this chapter — parental responsibilities, integrated social services, pre-school programs, urban and rural economic development. Some of these can be pursued by schools through local and regional partnerships if opportunities exist, as is the case in an increasing number of jurisdictions. We know that parental involvement and public support is essential for school success. In our own case studies of schools in Toronto, York Regional and Edmonton, we have found that involvement of parents and the community is the most difficult, least developed aspect of school improvement (Edge *et al.*, 2001, 2002, Mascall *et al.*, 2001).

There is another key point to be made. Parents have as much responsibility as do schools to combat disruptive student behavior and truancy. We often lay all the responsibility on teachers to compensate for poor family upbringing. David Miliband (2002), Minister of State for School Standards in England, states it dramatically in a speech to school principals:

> Governments have a responsibility to teachers but so do parents and the wider community. I have one simple message to you and anyone listening or watching: when it comes to parents, children or anyone else abusing teachers, the Government is 100 percent, unequivocally on your side.

There is one further, indirect point to be made about schools as professional learning communities. One of the interesting by-products of engaged learning communities is that they become more proactive with parents and the public. The dynamic, I think, is that when teachers are working alone, not learning together, they are not as confident about what they are doing (they literally may not know what they are doing). Lacking confidence in explaining themselves, and being on their own, they take fewer risks, play it safe, and close the classroom door. With the thirst for transparency on the part of the public (Lesson 5 in Chapter 3) this, of course, compounds the problem — making parents more suspicious, more insistent, and teachers more defensive.

By contrast, professional learning communities not only build confidence and competence, but they also make teachers and principals realize that they can't go the distance alone. These educators, inevitably, I would say, begin to reach out to and become more responsive to parent involvement and community development. This is a natural extension of learning systems, moral purpose and linking to the bigger picture through more engagement with the environment.

Complexity theory hammers home the point

One of the most advanced complexity theorists, Ralph Stacey at The Complexity and Management Centre, University of Hertfordshire, England, finds new knowledge and change deeply embedded in human interaction and relationships:

> Knowledge is always a process, and a relational one at that, which cannot therefore be located simply in an individual head, to be extracted and shared as an organizational asset. Knowledge is the act of conversing, and learning occurs when ways of talking, and therefore patterns of relationship change ... The knowledge assets of an organization, then, lie in the pattern of relationships between its members. (Stacey, 2001:98)

Later he observes:

> The future of an organization is perpetually constructed in the conversational exchanges of its members as they carry out their tasks. (p. 181)

Tipping Point, it will be recalled, produces changes when *groups* model new behavior (i.e., context changes). To see a group (such as teachers and the principal) act in new ways is to create a new context:

> If you want ... to bring about a fundamental change in people's belief and behavior, a change that would persist and serve as an example to others, you need to create a community around them, where these new beliefs could be practiced, expressed and nurtured. (Gladwell, 2000:173)

The new work on communities of practice is both theoretically and empirically confirmatory of the power of groups (Wenger, McDermott and Snyder, 2002:4):

> Companies at the forefront of the knowledge economy are succeeding on the basis of communities of practice, whatever they call them ...
>
> Communities of practice are groups of people who share a concern, a set of problems, or a passion about a topic, and who deepen their knowledge and expertise in this area by interacting on an ongoing basis ...

And

> A community of practice is a unique combination of three fundamental elements: a *domain* of knowledge, which defines a set of issues; a *community* of people who care about this domain; and the shared *practice* that they are developing to be effective in their domain. (p. 27, emphasis in original)

It is easy for communities of practice to become or be sterile. We talked earlier about Cohen and Hill's and McLaughlin and Talbert's findings that some professional communities have a great deal of exchange and even camaraderie but what they are doing is interacting to reinforce each other's ineffective practice (they don't know what they don't know). This means that communities of practice need to be conceptualized appropriately (to include, for example, diversity and the stimulus of outside ideas), and they must be constantly monitored and improved.

Wenger *et al.*, discuss the communities of practice activities of McKinsey & Company, the international management consultant group. Not only did McKinsey foster communities of practice as a way of organizational learning, they evaluated them as to their characteristics of effectiveness. All organizations operating effectively with complexity theory (whether they call it that or not) monitor and problem solve for efficacy. The assessment at McKinsey found two patterns related to less or more effectiveness.

The more effective practices produced a high energy cycle. Greater recognition, aspirations and effectiveness reinforced each other, which attracted highly committed people to the firm. The organizations with less effective practices were caught in a low energy cycle (Wenger *et al.*, 2002:164).

Wenger refers to these patterns as virtuous vs vicious cycles. For my purposes — "horizon #2" transformation — the only thing that works are virtuous cycles because they produce high energy up to the task of going deeper on a sustained basis. This is crucial:

> At the community level, the design philosophy is about eliciting the passion and participation of members. At the organization level, it is about combining this passion with the resources and power of the organization to create value far beyond what a community could achieve otherwise. (Wenger *et al.*, 2002:191)

You can't get this from the center or from heroic leaders. You need energy and the fostering of energy all over the place — what is called distributed leadership:

> Communities thrive on internal leadership. Similarly, knowledge organization depends on a distributed cadre of formal and informal leaders — both inside and outside communities — who have the vision and ability to help them reach their potential. (p. 192)

The point of knowledge development is to pursue the solution of hitherto unresolved organization problems. Wenger *et al.* (p. 190) discuss new initiatives at the World Bank which are organized around "thematic groups" focusing on such topics as community-based rural development, public health, urban upgrading, nutrition, and water resource management (one can think of action research groups playing a similar role in school systems). It doesn't end at developing new knowledge; there must be strategies for acting on it (like coaching, support groups and other forms of skill development).

Wenger *et al.* (2002:218) conclude:

> What is new about managing in the knowledge economy is the need to appreciate the tangible value of these intangible assets — passions, relationships, and skills — as much or more than the conventional assets listed on the ballot sheet.

When I compared businesses with education on these dimensions I found that (ironically, since schools are in the business of learning) top businesses are much more explicit about the role of knowledge in improvement than are educational systems (Fullan, 2001b). We need to correct this imbalance. Here are the main points as expressed by Brown and Duguid (2000):

- Knowledge lies less in its databases than in its people (p. 121)
- For all information's independence and extent, it is people, in their communities, organizations, and institutions, who ultimately decide what it all means and why it matters (p. 18)
- A viable system must embrace not just the technical system but also the social system — the people, organizations, and institutions involved (p. 60)
- Knowledge is something we digest rather than merely hold. It entails the knowers understanding and having some degree of commitment. (p. 120)

Brown and Duguid make the powerful point that information becomes knowledge only through a *social*, i.e., interactive, process:

> Attending too closely to information overlooks the social context that helps people understand what that information might mean and why it matters. (p. 5)
>
> Envisioned change will not happen or will not be fruitful until people look beyond the simplicities of information and individuals to the complexities of learning, knowledge, judgment, communities, organizations, and institutions. (p. 213)

If social interaction converts information into knowledge then sustained interaction produces wisdom.

Another powerful insight is that for a culture of knowledge sharing to exist it must be a two-way street. That is, there are two values acting in concert. One is the value that every individual in the organization is responsible for seeking new knowledge on a continuous basis; the other is that the same individuals are responsible for sharing what they know or contributing to the knowledge of others. The reason that this is key is that you won't get much of the former (adding new knowledge) if no one is sharing.

The essence of the theory is that you won't get deep change unless:

- People are interacting
- New knowledge is being produced in the heads of people
- New solutions are being discovered
- People own these solutions in the sense that they are passionately committed and energetic about pursuing them
- There are questioning and critical people so as to avoid locking into weak solutions and to continually seek potentially better ideas.

In short, there are two related reasons why we need these new cultures in school systems. One is that there is such a depth of knowledge required to go to new horizons that we can't possibly generate it without the ideas of teachers and principals coming to bear on complex problems. Second, we can't sustain the effort required unless local educators pour in their purpose, passion and concomitant energy.

It is hard to exaggerate how different the educational culture we are talking about is compared to what we now have. This is very deep change and will require a sophisticated mind and action set. Take, for example, the problem of order and control. Compare conditions of *laissez faire*, bounded collaboration, and the more complex intersystem collaboration I am talking about. *Laissez faire* systems have little discipline. They drift along in an inertial state and only a cataclysmic change in the environment disrupts their naïve complacency. Highly collaborative systems which are bounded (not connected to other systems) produce groupthink and possibly continuous uninformed change (as members interact and influence each other) which consolidates ever deeper *ineffective* practice.

But how can we have faith in non-linear, intersystem collaboration? The answer is (a) take a close look at whether current strategies are working, not only in relation to short-term results, but more importantly in relation to people's energy and passion — you will find that the present system de-motivates and de-energizes educators more than the opposite; and (b) to understand and use the powers of complexity theory.

On the issue of control, for example, complexity theories actually embody greater discipline than hierarchical systems. The social attractors in operation use ongoing interaction and the politics of support as control mechanisms. Stacey (1992) describes it this way:

> People learning in a group are displaying controlled behavior. Connections run from the discovery by individuals of small changes, anomalies, and ambiguities; to choice arising out of reflection, contention, and dialogue concerning the issues being discovered; to exploratory action; and back to discovery again as the processes of choice and the outcomes of exploratory actions provide further prompts to individual discoveries. Here behavior is constrained partly by individual differences in culture and perceptions and by disagreements that prevent a single view from dominating. Behavior is also partly constrained by the shared views that groups working together come to acquire, yet must constantly question if they are to learn. Constraint, then, is a consequence of the tension between

sharing and difference… People interacting politically are also displaying controlled behavior. Behavior is constrained by the unequal distribution of power, by the existence of hierarchy, and by the need to sustain sufficient support for views about issues and actions to be taken in regard to them. (pp. 165–6)

Hoban (2002) uses complexity theory to compare the inadequacies of the current system with what kind of system is needed for continuous teacher learning. He talks first about the mechanistic theory of educational change (the current culture):

When I reflect on my own life history as a high school teacher from 1976–1989, I believe I had a conception of teaching as a craft. I worked very hard in my first few years of teaching, learning science content, instructional strategies and classroom management techniques. Having acquired this level of expertise, I usually taught the same way year after year because I perceived that I had "mastered science teaching." … The legacy of my mechanistic conception of teaching as a craft was that I did not have a perceived need to constantly rethink how to improve my practice, rather I thought about how to consolidate it. (pp. 10–11)

Reflecting what we know about complexity theory, Hoban reminds us that a core feature of learning organizations is that they constantly ask and process troubling questions:

A sense of uncertainty or "intellectual unrest" is an inevitable consequence of being challenged, and is usually accompanied by confusion, uncertainty, anxiety, and stress. More importantly, such intellectual unrest is a necessary precursor to successful learning and thus, while often uncomfortable, plays a vital element in maintaining the energy level within the social system. (Hoban, 2002: 98)

Stacey (1992:120) made the same argument:

People do not provoke new insights when their discussions are characterized by orderly equilibrium, conformity, and dependence. Neither do they do so when their discussions enter the explosively unstable equilibrium of all-out conflict or complete avoidance of issues … People spark new ideas off each other when they argue and disagree — when they are conflicting, confused, and searching for new meaning — yet remain willing to discuss and listen to each other.

If you remember nothing else in this chapter, remember (because it is so easy to forget and to avoid) the kind of schools we are talking about confront reality and the inadequacies of the status quo — what Collins (2001) calls the ability to "confront the brutal facts yet never lose faith":

> Every good-to-great company [the 11 in his study] embraced [the following]: you must maintain unwavering faith that you can and will prevail in the end, regardless of the difficulties AND *at the same time* have the discipline to confront the most brutal facts of your current reality whatever they might be. (Collins, 2001:13, emphasis in original)

Collins compares "the doom loop" (innovations in typical organizations) with "the flywheel effect" that he found in the good-to-great companies. The doom loop sequence is:

- Disappointing results
- Reaction without understanding
- New direction, program leader, event, fad
- No build up; no accumulated momentum. (p. 179)

Whereas organizations with flywheel effect capacities face disappointing results and then:

- Step forward with what Collins calls "the hedgehog concept" (passion, best ideas, economic investment)
- Accumulate visible results
- People line up energized by results
- Flywheel builds further momentum. (p. 175)

Collins concludes:

> The good-to-great companies understood a simple truth: tremendous power exists in the fact of continued improvement and the delivery of results. (p. 174)

Alas, here is the kicker and key message of this chapter. Collins and his research team started with 1,435 companies selected from Fortune 500, 1965–1995 (in other words he sampled the best companies) and ended up with only *11 companies* that met the good-to-great criteria. We can conclude, then, about the first level of the tri-level question: the depth of change required must occur at this level but it rarely happens. That is what we are up against for starters.

In summary:

- Major new solutions are needed in schools
- There is great uncertainty about what they will look like and how to get there
- Uncertainty causes anxiety, which can have positive effects if channeled
- Successful organizations constantly ask themselves troubling questions, and are deliberately connected to external systems which do the same
- The social attractors enable them to ask and channel troubling questions in ways that produce good new ideas
- Accumulation of results energizes people to go even further.

We have now come full circle. All of what I have just said must occur on a massive scale. Schools can't get this good if left to their own devices, hence, the role of the infrastructure such as districts and states. While districts and states are *theoretically* important to this agenda, in empirical terms they have done more harm than good. On the edge of chaos test they have more often than not tipped us into chaos — multiple innovations colliding, policy churn as innovations come and go, piecemeal reform and an overall condition of overload and fragmentation. Some are over correcting by trying to impose too much order.

As to the argument that schools would be fine if the infrastructure would only leave them alone, forget it. It didn't happen in the past when there was the opportunity, it won't happen now. It can't. It is a theoretical certainty that we need *systems* (schools, districts, states) operating in interaction over time where they influence and learn from each other, improving their capacity not to panic in the face of disorder while they periodically consolidate the gains of new patterned breakthroughs. Two steps forward, one step back, and many steps sideways.

The test of the twenty-first century — a test for large-scale, sustainable reform — is whether districts and states can become more sophisticated complex systems, that can actually contribute to the development and fostering of new learning which is marked by the engagement and energy of the vast majority of educators and students as they obtain results never before accomplished. We need, in other words, very different districts and states than now exist.

Chapter 5

Tri-Level Reform: The Role of the District

The details are too important to leave to the devil.

Adapted from Block (2002:89)

Just as the school is hampered by the district, the district is hampered by the state. But let's do one hamper at a time. Put in a more balanced way, the tri-level argument is that each layer is helped or hindered by the layer above it (and each layer needs the commitment and energies of other layers in order to be successful). The school district, or local education authority, is one of the more interesting examples of auto-catalysis (how systems can learn from and influence each other).

The problem with studies of individual successful schools is that they treat the school as if it were an island. What if a given successful school was the only one like that or was in the distinct minority in its district. Worse still, what if that school became successful by robbing other schools of the best teachers thereby weakening the system as a whole. Since context has power, we need to change the context, and this means that the district as a system must change.

In this chapter we will take a look at the role of school districts in North America, consider briefly the district or local education authority in England where districts have less authority over individual schools and conclude with a segue to the role of the state.

It is time to introduce another distinction which has been only implicit up to this point, namely, the critical difference between having "a theory of education" and having "a theory of change" (or action). A theory of education includes the substance of content and pedagogy. In terms of this book it includes moral purpose and knowledge (in essence, Chapters 1 and 2). For example, a district that commits itself to improving literacy and closing the gap between high and low performers as it raises the bar chooses which literacy programs to go with (such as balanced literacy) on the basis of best knowledge. The district integrates moral purpose and knowledge to form its theory of education.

The theory of change, or action, concerns what policies, strategies and mechanisms are going to be used, in effect, to implement the theory of education (much of this book, of course, is about theories of change).

This may seem like a fine distinction but the two theories can co-exist independently of each other or one can be seriously underdeveloped at the expense of the other. Again, to take literacy, it is possible to be the world's leading expert on language development and simultaneously be a disastrous change agent.

When we do our training in school districts — most of which are focusing on literacy — we are developing the capacity of school teams and district staff to become more explicit about their change strategies: how to understand the change process; how to work with resistance; how to develop collaborative work cultures; how to find time; allocate resources; establish monitoring; develop leadership; and so on. All of these factors have nothing to do with literacy, and everything to do with the likelihood of its successful implementation. The districts develop their literacy expertise using internal and external resources as we work alongside them to help them integrate change strategies that make a difference in teacher and student learning.

Everyone has a theory of education and a theory of change however implicit, misguided, or underdeveloped it may be. My argument is that you cannot go deeply unless you create powerful new synergies between these two theories. Figure 5.1 summarizes the point.

The reason I introduce this distinction here is that as we move up the tri-levels, those leading the system need increasingly sophisticated conceptions of each set of theories, not, I must say to integrate them,

		Theory of education	
		Weak	Strong
Theories of change	Weak	Drift	Superficial change
	Strong	Change for the sake of change	Deep change

Figure 5.1 Theories of education and change

but to make them operate *seamlessly*. The higher the level — the more complex the change dynamics. Let's review some examples, which will show how complex these interactions really are. Remember, our complexity theory tells us that the goal is to enable one or more systems (such as schools) to interact with one or more other systems (such as districts) in order to mutually influence their respective capacities to learn and grow.

The role of the district

There are two sets of system relations at stake here. One is the state–district and the other is district–schools. We will place more emphasis in this chapter on the latter (taking into account the mediating role of the district in relation to state policy) with the former being taken up as part of Chapter 6. In the era of site-based management and central-ized accountability of the 1980s, local school districts almost fell out of the picture.

Districts are making a comeback; inevitably I would say, because of complexity theory (systems need systems, etc.). One need only compare the 2002 program of the American Education Research Association's Annual Meeting with the 2001 program to find the proliferation of sessions on the renewed role of the district. There are more districts that are active and much more research and evaluation being conducted (see Hightower *et al.*, 2002).

The vast majority of districts do not have the conception, capacity or continuity to be anything more than an episodic aggravation from the perspective of school effectiveness (what Hess (1999) has termed "spinning wheels and policy churn"). There are, as I have said, a growing number of active reform-oriented districts. I focus on these to show that some progress is being made, but also to make the point again that even in the best cases they are "horizon #1" successes (Chapter 1).

Memphis is an interesting case to start with. Memphis is Tennessee's largest school district, with 110,000 students and 161 schools. One in three children live in poverty; 83 percent are minority students (82 percent of whom are African-American); over 35 percent of the ninth-graders who start high school drop out before graduating. A new superintendent arrived in 1992 with a mandate for reform and started by gaining support among top leaders (the mayor, the business community, union leaders but, critically, not at the level of rank and file teachers). The superintendent's theory of education was to commit the district's schools to select among the seven whole school reform models sponsored by the New American Schools corporation (see Berends, Bodilly and Kirby, 2002).

It is difficult to extract the detailed theory of change in Memphis but it seems to include: rallying the support and resources of top leaders; a visionary exhortation to focus on moral purpose (closing the gap of learning); selection of "proven" external innovations which were comprehensive, and professional development and other forms of support to implement the selected models. In 1999, the super-intendent won the US National Superintendent of the Year Award. The superintendent had rapidly scaled up the number of schools adopting the reform models with 34 schools in the first cohort. By 1998, 75 of the 161 schools were involved with more being added.

Within a year of the 1999 award, the superintendent resigned. The new superintendent announced he was discontinuing the models and was quoted "if we could just stop experimenting and let the teachers teach" (Franceschini, 2002:2). Eight years of reform were discarded with hardly a tear. What went wrong?

The complete story is complicated, and I only use the case to illustrate some key points. The main problems in my view are:

- The reliance on external models: this is not to say that external models have no place, but they are not the main point; changing the culture of the profession is.
- Scaling up too quickly through the energy and commitment of a visionary pacesetter leader at the top.
- The corresponding neglect of the energy, intrinsic motivation and commitment of everyday teachers.

In 1998, an external research team had noted that while the reform initiative was highly touted that pervasively "teachers and principals express fatigue and feel unappreciated" (cited in Franceschini, 2002: 32). By 1999, feeling unheard, "hundreds of teachers jam ... school board headquarters ... to tell board members they're overworked and overwhelmed." The superintendent responded that "lagging test scores in city schools leave no room for the faint hearted" (p. 7). One teacher responded, "I love to teach — just let me do it" and was nearly drowned out by thundering applause from the audience.

Don't get me wrong. The "I love to teach" strategy has not delivered anything either. We are not talking about being soft on teachers, but rather about being more effectively demanding. More to the point is Elmore's (2003) argument:

Is it ethical to hold individuals — in this case educators — accountable for doing things they don't know how to do and can't be expected to do without considerable knowledge and skill ... (p. 6)

One possible answer is that it is not the school itself that is accountable but the sponsoring organization — the school system — that is accountable. (p. 5)

Elmore's point is that accountability systems which provide measures of student performance coupled with rewards and sanctions are necessary, but insufficient, because they omit strategies that would provide "the opportunity to acquire the new knowledge and skill necessary to produce the performance that is expected of them" (p. 7), what I have called "collective capacity-building."

One could argue that the professional development support associated with the whole school reform models does just that — give educators the wherewithal to make a difference. My answer is that it doesn't because it didn't. Or if you like, you can't get the kind of motivation we are talking about from external programs. You need to work on it directly by altering the working conditions of teachers in a way that makes it possible for them to improve and stay motivated on a sustained basis.

It is interesting to note that the New American Schools group has drawn the same conclusion. In reviewing its first ten years, NAS stresses that its focus is on comprehensive school improvement which it calls "A system approach, not just a design or model" (New American Schools, 2002:5). NAS is currently reconceptualizing its future to focus on leadership, school-wide reculturing and related fundamental changes at the school, community, district and state levels in order to achieve "system reform" to support continuous improvement.

District 2 in New York City is a second instructive example that is closer to the mark (but still with only horizon #1 results). District 2 has some 45 schools. In 1988 it ranked tenth among 32 community districts in the New York system in literacy and fourth in mathematics. By 1996, it ranked second on both. To get there District 2 used a combination of accountability and capacity-building strategies. Elmore and Burney (1999:26) describe the superintendent's (Anthony Alvarado) approach:

Over the eight years of Alvarado's tenure in District 2, the district has evolved a strategy for the use of professional development to improve teaching and learning in schools. This strategy consists of a set of organizing principles about the process of systemic change and the role of professional development in that process; in a set of specific activities, or models of staff development, that focus on systemwide improvement of instruction.

Elmore and Burney identified seven organizing principles of the reform strategy in District 2:

1. It is about instruction and only instruction
2. Instructional improvement is a long multi-stage process involving awareness, planning, implementation and reflection
3. Shared expertise is the driver of instructional change
4. The focus is on systemwide improvement
5. Good ideas come from talented people working together
6. Set clear expectations and then decentralize
7. Collegiality, caring and respect are paramount.

These principles have a lot more to them than the labels convey. Lesson 6, for example, contains a strong emphasis on central intervention in situations of persistent poor performance. Lesson 7 has a strong degree of pressure. Be that as it may, to the extent that leaders at all levels of the system internalize and act on these seven principles, instructional improvements and student learning will be enhanced as they were in District 2.

The underlying conception is critical and very difficult to transfer. To make the point, let us consider two additional cases, Baltimore and San Diego. The Baltimore City public school system has a concentration of low-performing schools. Through an intensive intervention strategy, the District turned around the eighteen poorest performing schools in the central part of the city. Within three years (1998–2001), reading scores in terms of median national percentiles more than doubled (Dicembre, 2002:33).

Baltimore accomplished this impressive feat by combining three strategies: a balanced literacy program (theory of education), intense professional development in relation to the program, and continuous monitoring and feedback — the latter two, if you like, being part of a theory of change. Now, my question is: does this provide the basis for continuous and deeper improvement? We don't know the answer, but some of the elements consistent with the themes we have been pursuing can be identified.

First, Baltimore educators could be justifiably proud and further motivated by their accomplishments, building on the moral purpose of doing good. Second, and on the other hand, we don't know from the article how teachers and principals in those schools feel — about the pace of reform, their own ownership *vis-à-vis* centrally driven reform, and so on. Third, do those leading the strategy have a deep conception of what they are doing? Say, at least deep enough to encompass the seven organizing principles we just discussed.

All of this is to question the depth of the change. It is possible to take policy pieces (a program, professional development, monitoring), implement them well and get good short-term results without understanding the deeper conceptions related to creating first-rate learning communities. My argument is that deep and sustained change is related to whether scores of educators, especially those in leadership positions, come to hold and strengthen core underlying conceptions. The power lies in the conceptions, not in the surface policy levers.

A more interesting case is the San Diego City Schools District because many of the same strategies from District 2 have been introduced with a greater sense of urgency in a larger, more complex system. San Diego has 142,000 students and 180 schools — a third of the students are Latino, quarter Caucasian, a fifth African-American, and the remainder Asian or other.

The superintendent is Alan Bersin, a former California state attorney who on his appointment in 1998 immediately hired Anthony Alvarado as chancellor of instruction (equivalent to a superintendent). San Diego is being watched carefully as evidenced in several research evaluations focusing on the experiences and performance of the system (The American Institutes for Research, 2002; Darling-Hammond, 2002; Hightower, *et al.*, 2002; McLaughlin and Talbert, 2001; Stein, Hubbard and Mehan, 2002).

Again the story is exceedingly complex and I can only use it to illustrate some of the dilemmas of large-scale, sustainable reform. Prior to the Bersin–Alvarado arrival, San Diego was a typical urban district of the kind that caught Tom Hatch's interest when multiple innovations collide. From one perspective it was a highly innovative district — except that the initiatives were fragmented and came and went in irregular patterns. Projectitis prevailed; there was little to show for all the efforts; there was no impact on student learning — lots of footwork, little traction.

In short order, Bersin and Alvarado announced:

> The mission of San Diego City Schools is to improve achievement by supporting teaching and learning in the classroom. Within this goal was a focus on the lowest performing students and schools as a means to raise the overall performance so as to build districtwide unity of purpose. (Hightower, 2002:123)

In year 1 (1998–9), they dramatically changed the structure of the district office from one in which feeder schools (40 or more schools) were organized into five area superintendencies to a structure organized around eight "instructional leaders" (ILs) whose job it was to work with 25 schools each to help principals and teachers focus on instruction and student achievement, especially in literacy and mathematics. Only one of the five area superintendents became one of the eight instructional leaders as Bersin and Alvarado hired and trained this new leadership cadre.

Bersin and Alvarado believed that the area superintendency structure "bred inequities and fiefdoms and lacked orientation to systemwide instructional needs" (Hightower, 2002:124). Whereas:

> In contrast to former area superintendents, the ILs worked closely together, co-constructing their new roles and jointly planning their coaching work with principals. In addition they collectively received specialized training. (p. 125)

The instructional system in San Diego is reflected in the District's main document, the *Blueprint for Student Success in a Standards-Based System* (San Diego City Schools District, 2000). The *Blueprint* is supported by a well worked out set of instructional practices such as the literacy framework with a focus on student learning, a vastly improved data system to monitor and act on student achievement results, professional development directed at instructional improvement, and so on. Professional development for principals, teachers, peer-coach staff developers, instructional leaders, is systematically built into monthly, weekly and daily interactions organized around the concept of "nested learning communities" (Fink and Resnick, 2001).

Hightower provides a sense of the focus and intensity of the new system:

> Alvarado and the ILs devised structures through which principals could learn about exemplary instructional practice and ways to support teacher and student learning. Foremost among these were required monthly principals conferences ... these meetings established regular occasions for Learning Communities to convene and for principals and district administrators to discuss reform implementation ... (p. 125)
>
> A second primary mechanism for principal learning was called "Walkthrough", a school accountability and review process adapted from District 2 to evaluate site progress and assist principals in identifying instructional support needs. (p. 126)

By the start of the reform's second year nearly 100 certified and trained literacy peer coaches blanketed two-thirds of district schools ... coaches spent four days a week at the school sites. On the fifth day [central] staff ... helped coaches understand their roles and the instructional strategies that teachers were beginning to implement. (pp. 130–1)

Bersin and Alvarado's theories of instruction and change were specific. They explicitly identify their instructional theory as an attempt to professionalize teaching by grounding decisions in both greater shared knowledge about effectiveness practice and an expectation that teachers will learn to apply knowledge to the individual needs of students (Darling-Hammond, 2002:14).

We have seen that Bersin and Alvarado use an intensive centrally driven professional development and support system to drive the reform. Unlike District 2 where the strategy grew organically, San Diego used what Hightower calls the "Big Boom" approach. Bersin used the word "jolt":

There was no other way to start systemic reform. You don't announce it. You've got to jolt the system. I understand that ... If people don't understand you're serious about change in the first six months the bureaucracy will own you. The bureaucracy will defeat you at every turn if you give it a chance. (Hightower, 2002:121)

I said in Chapter 3 that you cannot get large-scale reform through bottom-up strategies; the question I pose here is: what are the tensions and consequences of a more centrally driven approach? Note I am not talking about motives, but rather about consequences. Alvarado, in the interview I conducted in 2001, made his intentions clear:

We are in our third year. I see and feel that there has been a definite shift to implement the reform. We started with a strong district plan. We wanted to get principals to understand that we have created district parameters. But this initiative is not about simply implementing a district plan. It is about drawing out what principals stand for. Granted, it is not about doing your own thing, but I also don't want principals to follow a procedural plan. I want them to ask "How do I develop a culture in my school that gets people to understand what they can do together to help students?" I am interested in the hearts and minds of principals. The feeling is that something is being done to them, but that is not our intent. We are creating a system for them to take responsibility, for them to understand internally how they can commit deeply to student learning. I actually think that instructional leadership, when it is done well, is transformational leadership. (Interview, January 29, 2001)

What has been the impact of San Diego's big boom strategy? First, concerning student achievement data both AIR and Hightower note that student achievement scores have increased year by year but are cautious about causal attribution. Shortly I will ask the question: assume that there are some real gains; have they set the stage for further development or its opposite?

Second, principals, reports Hightower, are mostly enthusiastic about the changes. They appreciate the new role and support of instructional leaders. They value the walkthroughs, monthly conferences and "spoke enthusiastically about the reforms equalizing quality" with all schools getting the same message and striving for greater consistency (Hightower 2002: 137). AIR evaluators also report "positive reactions to the provision of enhanced resources and rich offerings of professional development" (American Institutes of Research, 2002, vi). Principals surveyed in the AIR study reported a major and valuable change in their roles toward becoming instructional leaders. Darling-Hammond's (2002) survey indicates very high ratings from elementary school principals about various professional development components with middle and high school principals less enthused.

Third, San Diego also revamped its personnel office to focus on the recruitment and support of new teachers putting the entire system on line with improved capacity for seeking and responding to new applicants. Darling-Hammond (2002:17) observes:

> By the fall of 2002, while districts like San Francisco and Los Angeles hired hundreds of uncredentialed teachers and the state as a whole hired more than 50 percent of beginners without full credentials, San Diego filled almost every one of its 1,081 vacancies with fully qualified teachers.

This is a crucial and often neglected point. Most districts have poor hiring practices and weak support for beginning teachers. By focusing on these aspects, districts can drastically reduce both the hiring of uncredentialed teachers and the attrition rate of beginning teachers (say, for example, from an average of 30 percent of beginning teachers not lasting more than four years, to five percent). For a smaller district that has made a virtue of doing this see Snyder's (2002) case study of New Haven Unified School District in California.

All of the above are positive, but there is a flip side. Teachers have appreciated the emphasis on professional development and the new role of the principal, but disagreed with the method and pace of implementation of the reform — "too cut-throat", "too top-down", "bureaucratic" (Hightower, 2002:138). Principals also spoke "about feeling overworked and somewhat fearful about the pressures and consequences for principals and school performance under the new district administration" (Darling-Hammond, 2002:35).

AIR evaluators go a step further in talking about a climate of fear and suspicion among school staff in which: "teachers report that they are exhausted, stressed out, and in some cases fearful of losing their jobs if they do not perform under this new program" (American Institutes of Research, 2002:x). Many teachers have complained that their input has not been sought about the direction of the reform. The union leadership (San Diego Education Association) opposed the method of the reform virtually from the beginning and has remained a strong source of opposition.

On balance, one would have to conclude that San Diego's reform is fragile as of its fourth year. There is strong support from the majority of principals, and many teachers like the content of much of the reform activities, but object to the method and pace of implementation and their lack of input. Politically it is fragile. Bersin was appointed by the school board in 1998 with a slim majority. Student achievement results, climate in the organization, the role of top leaders in the business community, and parent and teacher leaders will all figure in determining the likelihood of the reform continuing. To be clear, an enormous amount has been accomplished in a very short period. The question is about the reform's continued viability.

Our complexity theorists would have a field day with San Diego as it cycles in and around the edge of chaos and the edge of order. To consolidate:

- Most districts operate desultory systems closer to chaos than order.
- Greater coherence is thus needed — integration must occur around the three policy levers identified by Cohen and Hill (2001) (curriculum, assessment and teacher learning).
- San Diego has employed these three levers in a systematic way.
- If the center tries to extract too much order it runs the risk of alienating, burning out, or otherwise disaffecting too many teachers.
- Put another way, as the strategy unfolds leaders must pay close attention to whether they are generating passion, purpose and

energy — intrinsic motivation — on the part of principals and teachers. Failure to gain on this problem is a sure-fire indicator that the strategy will fail sooner than later.

- The way to gain on the purpose/passion/energy syndrome is to improve one's strategy as it unfolds (all effective complex systems have responsive feedback and problem-solving capacities in relation to other systems they are interacting with).

Timing is also an issue. It may be necessary in chaotic systems to start more forcefully and adjust later. There is some evidence that this is happening in San Diego. In response to one survey which showed that high school principals were much less connected with the district's strategy (39 percent agreed that "the district does not understand my school's reform agenda" compared to only six percent of elementary school principals), district leaders have reorganized learning communities to create two high-school-only groups with principals playing a role in developing new directions.

To conclude, I return to the question I posed earlier: Let us assume that the student achievement gains are real. This is not success if it cannot be sustained and deepened. There is some evidence that tightly controlled strategies can get short-term gains, but this will not take us to the new horizons discussed in Chapter 1. In fact, it could be that such strategies reduce the chances of going further as they burn out teachers. New, more powerful policies and practices are needed to go beyond what we are now witnessing in even the seemingly most successful districts.

A very brief trip to England

Districts or local education authorities (LEAs) are different in England. The 1988 Education Reform Act introduced different degrees of governance in schools with devolution of authority and finances along with centralization of standards and accountability (Bennett, Anderson and Wise, 2002). Each school has its own board of governors. The LEAs, on the average, are much larger than districts in the USA, often having 100 or more schools, some much larger.

There was some speculation in the 1990s that LEAs would be abolished altogether. With the election of the Labour Government in 1997, a code of practice was established concerning the relationships of schools to LEAs in which the relative autonomy of schools is recognized. In addition to support (i.e., non-authority roles), the main proactive role of LEAs is captured in the phrase "intervention in inverse proportion to success," i.e., LEAs should intervene in the case of failing schools. In any case, LEAs in England have much less authority than their counterparts in North America.

The new role of the LEA in England remains ambiguous, but I offer the case as an example of spontaneous patterns emerging as systems interact around moral purpose and knowledge sharing. We saw in Chapter 2 that districts in some of England's poorest cities have made the largest gains in student achievement over the past five years (despite not having the same degree of authority, as is the case in the US).

My point is that there are a variety of ways in which systems can organize themselves to bring together curriculum, assessment and teacher learning. Some of these in England include twinning schools to work together, and other intra-LEA or across LEA partnerships. Still others have entire LEAs and all their schools developing together even though there is no formal requirement that they do so.

The moral purpose of closing the gap in achievement can be an added rallying point for collaborative efforts. New horizons, moral purpose, the eight lessons for complex change all provide compelling rationales and ideas for interaction with external entities and larger networks. System transformation requires that all levels see themselves as part and parcel of a larger learning enterprise.

Segue to the role of the state

So far I have focused on district–school relationships. Districts also find themselves contending with state policy. What does this look like from the perspective of the district (the state's perspective is taken up in the next chapter)?

One recent study of mathematics reform in Michigan in nine districts is revealing (Spillane, 2003). Once again we confront the superficial versus deeper aspects of reform. Just as teachers need to learn, so do the district staff who are expected to lead the reforms at the local level. Spillane found that in the majority of cases, district leaders operated in what he called a "quasi-behaviorist" manner, i.e., they saw themselves as transmitting new knowledge to teachers. Moreover, district leaders operating in this role did not themselves have a deeper understanding of the conceptions underlying the mathematics reform.

By contrast, district leaders operating from a "quasi-cognitive" perspective were more likely to grasp the underlying conceptions of the reform, seek greater alignment of curriculum assessment, and establish more intensive teacher learning experiences; whereas the quasi-behaviorists believed in external motivation (rewards and sanctions) the quasi-cognitivists sought learning experiences with teachers that would be more grounded in their day-to-day work and learning, leading to greater understanding and commitment on the part of teachers.

So, point number one is that districts do matter but at the present most of them appear to be weak agents in the reform triage.

Point number two is that proactive districts can use state policy to leverage and integrate their reform initiatives (this is an important tri-level generalization: systems working with moral purpose and seeking greater knowledge should see themselves as "exploiting" other levels to achieve these ends as they learn from their exchanges).

Darling-Hammond (2002) describes how this works in San Diego:

> From a bottom-up or inside-out perspective, we might say that the district's strategies must contend with policy interventions and conditions from the state level that may either impede or support reform initiatives ... district leaders in San Diego leverage, mediate, translate or ignore state policies to further the instructional improvement goals of the district. (p. 25)

The district was able to use funds from the state's Beginning Teacher Support and Assessment (BTSA) program to augment and integrate the peer coaching infrastructure for literacy; the literacy framework served as an "anchor" to interpret state reading policies; the district served as a buffer with respect to the state's accountability measures by intervening on behalf of the schools under threat of state takeover by proactively developing a plan for those schools. And so on.

Most districts do not have their act together to the point where they could serve as a coherence-maker in linking schools and state policies. And some may be too good at blunting the intent of state reform. Our complexity theory argument, of course, is that these relationships cannot be tightly controlled, but rather that we should invest in capacity development at all levels, open up lines of interaction across and within levels, monitor performance, and look for and consolidate promising patterns and gains.

This makes the state's role exceedingly complex — the last of our tri-level partners.

Chapter 6

Tri-Level Reform: The State

The edge of chaos is a sexy term, but we could just as easily call it the edge of order. They are the same thing. Governments will find it more palatable to think in terms of the edge of order. The mindset is to promote/allow variety, to use and trust the social attractors of moral purpose, quality relationships and quality ideas to generate and extract new patterns and gains.

Working with complexity theory is a difficult proposition for policy-makers because the general public looks for clarity of leadership, and results (although, as we saw earlier from Bricker and Greenspon's (2001) analysis, the public is capable of much greater informed judg-ment). It would be folly, not to mention a contradiction in terms, for policymakers to attempt to apply complexity theory literally. What would be appropriate is to use the ideas from the theory to guide policy and strategies of implementation.

In this chapter I illustrate this line of thinking in three ways. First by reviewing the eight lessons for complex change from Chapter 3 from the perspective of a policymaker (Figure 3.1). This won't be the whole story but it will give us ideas about how to apply complexity thinking. Second, I will offer a theory of education which itself is compatible with complexity theory. This will set the stage for making policy suggestions for how to make this theory of education come to life. So, in order: eight lessons, a theory of education, policies for getting there.

The eight lessons

The first of the eight lessons is give up the idea that the pace of change will slow down. For a policymaker this means not making promises that can't be kept. Most educators will not experience a slow down in the pace of change in any case. But policymakers can work on alignment, coherence and reducing distracting requirements (such as bureaucratic paperwork). They can promise a move towards greater coherence and an investment in capacity-building that would enable educators to achieve greater integration and reduce the negative effects of piecemeal change. It is not the pace of change that needs to slow down, but rather the misalignment and incoherence of reforms should be reduced.

The second lesson follows: coherence making is everyone's responsibility. The policymaker's responsibility is threefold. Make a good start by aligning policies at the center (such as curriculum, assessment, teacher learning); relentlessly talk with local educators about "the big picture," listen to their concerns and strive for ever greater clarity; provide opportunities for local educators to connect outside themselves — make it clear that "connecting the dots" is everyone's responsibility.

Lesson three, changing contexts means that you do not confine the policy set to individual incentives and sanctions, but you announce that a change in conditions is also a primary goal. For example, practices to reduce unnecessary workload, policies that foster professional learning networks and communities which provide new contexts à la "tipping points" (Gladwell, 2000).

The fourth lesson concerns premature clarity. For both substantive and tactical reasons too much front-end clarity is a bad idea. Relative to the former, there are too many unknowns for complex solutions to be predetermined. To a certain extent you have to work them out by doing them and you need the ideas of front line implementers to do this. The tactical reason concerns the politics of implementation and ownership. People will have greater ownership because they are contributing ideas and because they are involved. This doesn't mean that leaders should be deliberately vague. One can be clear and inspiring about the goals and the direction, and then set up more flexible strategies and processes for getting there (which often ends up redefining some of the goals). For complex change the job description is one of finding clarity, not implementing it.

Lesson five — the public thirst for transparency — means that policymakers cannot backtrack on making information available even though it is sometimes misused. There are judgments to be made about the overuse of targets and league tables, but student performance data should be made readily available to educators and the public. The emphasis should be on improving the capacity of educators and the broader public to interpret and use achievement data — to become more "assessment literate" — and to seek additional measures of performance.

Lesson six, use large-scale reform strategies but beware of the trap of teacher dependency or alienation. Policymakers using this guideline would first put in place a systematic strategy for literacy and numeracy. Part of the initial goal is to take quick action (it still takes a few years) in order to raise the floor of student achievement, close the gap between high and low performers and raise the bar of achievement. The other part of the goal is to help develop the capacity of local educators to move beyond centrally driven reform. Sooner rather than later, start announcing your intentions to, and create policies and mechanisms for, inviting and supporting ideas from teachers and principals — compatible, of course, with policy directions. Realize and state that capacity and ownership of local educators is the only thing that counts in the mid to long term.

Lesson seven helps address the Achilles heel of centrally directed reform. The goal is to convert teacher, principal and district skepticism into commitment and ownership. Articulating and working with the social attractors of moral purpose, quality relationships and quality knowledge is essential in the conversion process.

Finally, lesson eight means that as you focus on leadership development as a key, don't take shortcuts. A few good leaders won't do it. A few, seemingly great leaders, may do more harm than good if they inhibit the development of others. In policies and inquiry, focus as much on the conditions and processes of leadership succession as you do on the preparation and support of new leaders.

This quick review of the eight lessons is not meant to be the whole story for policymakers, but rather to loosen up the mindset and give a flavor of complexity thinking. It is crucial to stress that complexity theory is systemic, that is, the eight lessons operate *in interaction* providing internal checks and balances. To put it directly, if you use any one of the lessons in isolation you will end up making mistakes; by using the eight in combination you *can't* make a mistake, or more accurately, what mistakes are made are inevitably corrected because the very processes guarantee it. The next section provides more assurance for those looking for something systematic.

A generic theory of education

If you take the ideas and themes of the previous five chapters and put them in their most succinct form, you come up with Figure 6.1.

In the center are the three policy levers that Cohen and Hill (2001) identified in their study of mathematics reform in California. They found that strong results were obtained when the new curriculum (defined comprehensively to include conceptual frameworks, instruction, materials), ongoing assessment of student work, and opportunities

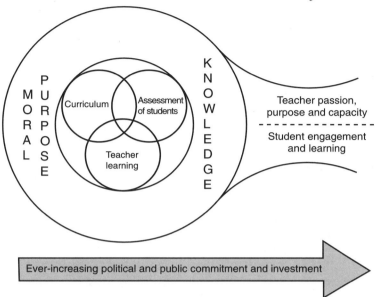

Figure 6.1 Generic theory of education

for teacher learning were aligned as experienced by teachers over an intense period of learning. The problem was that only one in ten teachers had such experiences. Surrounding the inner three circles is moral purpose and quality knowledge to connote, respectively, that making a difference/reducing the gap must be a constant preoccupation (or, more accurately, an occupation), and that new ideas from other teachers and from other external experts must be continuously processed to improve what is being attempted.

Arising from these experiences is deep engagement on the part of teachers and students. If tests scores go up and engagement doesn't deepen, improvement will be superficial and unsustainable. Note in Figure 6.1 that I have placed teacher passion, capacity, and ownership as co-equal to student engagement and learning. The logician, and even the moralist, may object, since teacher efficacy is a means to the more important goals of student learning. The complexity strategist would also agree literally but would say that teacher capacity is so easily missed in present circumstances that we had better highlight it. By so doing we are likely to take it more seriously and, paradoxically, far from downplaying the student we actually increase the chances that students will be better off (because it is only through the committed efforts of the entire teaching force that we can move forward).

Figure 6.1 is generic so that there are a lot of details omitted including the surrounding conditions and policies that would be necessary, but it is a pretty good overview. It also embeds complexity doubly. First, the internal dynamics of the model are complexity-congruent in the sense that when complexity works to most advantage, it immerses all actors in intensive interaction, new learnings and deeper commitments to each other and the goals they are pursuing. Complexity theory is also implicated in a deeper way. You need to know a lot about it in order to address the bigger complexity question. How do you get there?

Policies for getting there

Right off the mark we face a Catch 22. We need deep commitment and capacities on the part of teachers and principals for Figure 6.1 to work effectively, but in most cases we don't have them to start with. Most responses to this dilemma bypass or beg the question, introduce policies that are insufficient for the task, or fall back on the romantic folly of "if only" thinking (such as if only we left teachers alone and let them teach).

Instead what we need are a set of informed policies, and complexity thinking policymakers who are prepared to engage in the heavy interactive dynamics of implementing the direction of these policies in an iterative manner. This results in greater and greater engagements of educators, parents and the community, and students. In this section I indicate three sets of policies that are needed and use the case of England to take up the deeper dynamics of what is involved — both in terms of policy and action — for moving from where we are now to new horizons.

Before taking up the education policies it should be noted that policy reform in other sectors is an essential part of the success equation. Rothstein (2002) makes a compelling case that we rely too heavily on school interventions and fail to implicate other institutions:

> Because families, communities, and social policies all have an impact on student achievement, programs to raise student achievement should not assume that the only way of doing so is with better school policies. A variety of interventions — social, economic, and instructional — should compete for attention and resources as means of raising student achievement. (p. 25)

In any case there are three interrelated sets of education policies that are needed. Figure 6.2 incorporates the policy set in Figure 6.1

into a more comprehensive model which includes policies aimed at individual development and at improving working conditions.

As I illustrate each set, keep in mind two things: (a) high quality policy and implementation of each set are required; and (b) the impact of each set of policy levers will be weakened unless interaction and learning are occurring across the policies (see Figure 6.2),

One policy set involves the particular curriculum that constitutes what students should learn, how it should be assessed, and what teacher learning is required for the first two to happen. I have noted before that these policies must be aligned at the state level and implemented in a way that teachers experience the alignment as they work through new practices and beliefs. The literacy and numeracy strategy in England is a good example of quality policy in the first set (see Barber, 2002). Cohen and Hill's (2001) account of mathematics reform in California is also a good example of the potential alignment, although in this particular case, policymakers failed to address alignment at the level of implementation. I have also said there is much more work to be done in this policy set, because so far the best examples are confined to literacy and mathematics. More comprehensive and fundamental learning goals remain to be

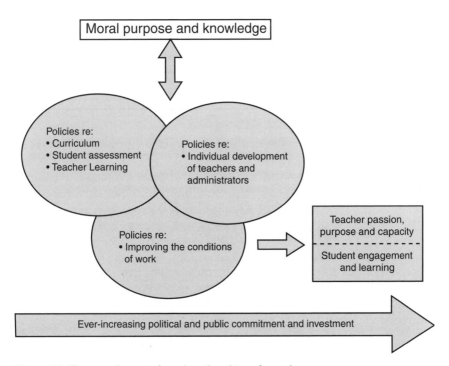

Figure 6.2 Three policy sets for educational transformation

addressed; nonetheless, moving forward in this policy area is the point.

The second and third sets are more fundamental, and more generic in the sense that they don't refer to a specific curriculum but to the ongoing development of the basic capacities of educators and the conditions under which they work. Moreover, the key point is that you cannot go deep in the first policy set without major support from the other two. Let's illustrate.

Policy set 2 — related to the individual development of teachers and administrators — concerns policy to strengthen in fundamental ways the teaching profession (including administrators). We have already seen an excellent example of this set, namely, Connecticut, although it should be acknowledged that the task is more complex and daunting in some states than others; the problems in California, for example, are considerably more challenging (California Commission on Teachers Credentialing, 1997, and Shields *et al.*, 2001). Over the period of a decade, Connecticut developed and implemented a comprehensive set of policies, which dramatically improved the teaching profession in that state. The Education Amendment Act and associated legislation:

- Raised and equalized teacher salaries across districts, providing state salary aid to reach a target minimum for the salaries of fully certified teachers;
- Increased licensing standards requiring more teacher training at entry, including: a major in the field to be taught; more focused study of learning and teaching; greater preparation to teach special needs learners; and the passage of basic skills and content tests;
- Enacted scholarships and forgivable loans (financial loans to newly hired teachers that do not require payback if the teacher remains in the position for a specified period of time) to attract high ability candidates into teaching at undergraduate and graduate levels and to encourage candidates to teach in priority schools and subjects with teacher shortages;
- Facilitated entry for well-trained teachers from out-of-state;
- Eliminated emergency licensing;
- Toughened requirements for temporary licenses, granting them only for teachers seeking a second license or endorsement, or entering from out-of-state;
- Created a staged licensing process that included a beginning teacher program for all new teachers and a master's degree for securing a professional license;

- Required and funded trained mentors for all beginning and student teachers;
- Required ongoing professional development for a professional license (30 credits at the graduate level, later increased to a master's degree) and for license renewal (nine credits every five years); and
- Required districts to develop professional development plans, career incentives plans, and teacher evaluation systems, and then partially funded implementation of the plans, plus evaluation and dissemination of the most effective models. (Wilson *et al.*, 2001:9)

The result has been that the shortage of qualified teachers in urban areas in Connecticut has been transformed to surpluses statewide; districts with sharply improved achievement levels cited the high and steadily increasing quality of teachers and administrators as a critical reason for their gains; the number of teachers holding masters degrees is almost double the national average, and so on.

As for student achievement, student gains in reading for fourth-graders in the 1992–8 period outstripped all other states in the nation:

Fourth-graders' scores grew significantly over time, leaving Connecticut in a class of its own … The proportion of students scoring at or above the proficient level in reading moved from 34 percent to 46 percent (as compared to the 1998 national average of 29 percent). Eighth graders also met or surpassed student performance in all other states. (Wilson *et al.*, 2001:28)

As with all good policies, this is steady, hard work. All effective policy sets are underpinned by sophisticated conceptions of a qualified and effective future teaching profession, investments in quality implementation, and feedback mechanisms for improving the policies as they unfold:

The state's comprehensive teacher policies have provided a base of professional expertise for all of its other reforms … Connecticut's particular brand of low-stakes, standards-based reform has tied increasingly authentic, information-rich assessments to analytic supports for districts and schools seeking to understand their achievement patterns as well as to curriculum improvements targeted to those needs and to professional development in support of curriculum change. (p. 31)

And,

> The story of Connecticut's reform is one of focused, purposeful capacity-building throughout the educational system, driven by pointed attention to teaching quality and the creative use of available state policy levers ...
>
> We believe that the "package" of policies — any one of which is insufficient when used in isolation — helped create a culture that valued teachers and teaching, enabled the acquisition and ongoing development of professional knowledge among educators, and held those educators to high standards ... Examined over time, this array of constantly unfolding policies is an unusual story of large-scale, iterative, system-wide, state-wide reform. (p. 32)

The necessity of policymakers creating feedback and problem-solving mechanisms throughout implementation is critical:

> Meanwhile, CSDE [Connecticut State Department of Education] staff also set about learning from their own experiences. Their commitment to data, research and inquiry foreshadowed the current national trend pressing educators to ground assessment and data. All along, as instruments were being pilot-tested and implemented, the research and evaluation division conducted reliability and validity studies that were then, in turn, critically used in the redesign of policy. Staff members presented their analyses and experiences to policymakers, parents and research, locally and nationally. They invited criticism and commentary and they willingly tinkered with or transformed practices that were ineffective or inefficient ...
>
> This kind of pedagogical stance — of inquiring instead of pronouncing, of encouraging dialogue rather than silencing participants — is strikingly different from most policy implementation. (p. 33)

Policymakers learning, a fundamental premise of complexity thinking (systems learning from each other) is something that only a few governments have cottoned onto.

In effect, Connecticut has done an effective job of employing and integrating the first two policy sets. There is still more to be done such as establishing arm's length teaching councils (similar to law societies and medical associations) which have legislative authority over monitoring and guiding teacher development — the Ontario Council of Teachers in Canada, the General Teaching Councils in Scotland and in England are examples. Nonetheless, Connecticut has made an impressive start in policy area two.

Connecticut has indirectly affected the third set — the hidden killer of educational transformation — the failure of policymakers to address the working conditions of teachers. We cannot nearly get to "horizon #2" unless we develop an integrated policy set for altering the conditions under which teachers and principals work. As a transition to the third policy set, let's take a moment to indicate why the second set is insufficient to carry the day. To overstate it slightly: never send a changed individual into an unchanged environment! Of course, I would not say never literally, but if you look closely at the second policy set it focuses on *individual* development of teachers and administrators and that's all right as far as it goes. You could say it indirectly affects the organization, because individuals with new capacities will add up, but why limit it to this strategy? Besides, individual development by itself will never bring the system transformation we are talking about. You also need, in other words, companion policies that directly focus on altering *the system*.

This third policy set has not been tried anywhere on a large scale but is now being considered. It is crucial for reaching horizon #2. The British government commissioned PriceWaterhouseCoopers (2001) to conduct a study of the working conditions of teachers both in isolation and in comparison with those in business and industry. PWC concluded that the current conditions in schools were hostile to creating the capacity for making improvements in a sustainable way. Their analysis led them to recommend the following types of changes:

1. Reduce the workload of teachers and principals, especially in relation to paperwork and tasks that take teachers away from teaching or that could be done by others.
2. Increased, guaranteed non-contact time for teachers in the school day so that they can work together.
3. Add more teaching assistants and make better use of all support staff in schools.
4. Improve the way governments introduce and support change, communicate with and monitor schools.

This is not the full list and it certainly is not one for the faint-hearted. It would be easy to pass formal policies in these domains that end up squandering public money. I will say, however, that it is critical to tackle this policy set because it is the last frontier for bringing the teaching profession into the twenty-first century. Common advice among horse trainers is that if the horse you are riding is dead, it is a good idea to get off. The traditional organization of the school is education's dead horse.

It is obvious that we are talking about the most complex change of any in this book. What will be required are policymakers who have a strong underlying conception of the future role of public schools (which in effect is the conception that underpins and cuts across the three policy sets), and who are adept at complexity theory and practice, i.e., at working through the politics of capacity-building.

I don't mean to imply that policymakers have to go it alone. Leadership will be required at all levels including, for example, from union leaders who, among other things, will have to become more open about the use of teaching assistants. But this is a chapter for policymakers and they are in the best position to push in this direction as they tap into leaders at other levels with similar interests and as they create the maximum blend of accountability and capacity-building (see Elmore, 2002b).

Not the least of the initial dilemmas is the Catch 22 problem I referred to earlier. How do you invest in capacity without wasting resources if schools do not have the capacity to use the resources effectively in the first place? Elmore (2003:28) puts it this way:

> To lay new resources on school systems, without requiring them to reallocate their own resources toward improvements in capacity is to reinforce their own prior inefficiencies.

Elsewhere Elmore states:

> The fact that most school systems do not already have a coherent and powerful professional development system is, itself, evidence that they would not know what to do with increased professional development funding. Investing in more professional development in low capacity, incoherent systems is simply to put more money into an infrastructure that is not prepared to use it effectively. Thus, the question of capacity precedes and coexists with the question of how much new money should be invested in professional development. (Elmore, 2002b:23)

All of this is to say that you need to know a great deal about complex change forces to lead and stay alive in this arena (Heifetz and Linsky, 2002). A case example will illustrate the kind of thinking I am talking about and will give us hope that there is great potential for breakthroughs.

Getting there: case illustration

I take England as the example because there are deliberations going on about how to move forward on the third policy set while strengthening the first two sets. In May 2002, we conducted all-day workshops in each of eight different local educational authorities (LEAs) across England. There were about 80 participants on the average, comprising heads of schools, deputy heads, LEA staff, and some teachers. The workshops focused on understanding the change process, building professional learning communities, closing the gap in student achievement, the roles of schools, LEAs and government, and leadership requirements. Among other matters we talked about the prescription–autonomy and the knowledge poor–rich dimensions (recall Figure 1.2). We asked the participants to respond to two open-ended questions:

1. What are the obstacles to moving from informed prescription to informed professional judgment?
2. What strategies would you suggest for moving in this direction.

We told the respondents that we would be advising the government on these matters.

Thus, we have, in their own words, the ideas of over 600 local educators from across the country including two LEAs that are part of the greater London system. This is clearly not a random sample. Local leaders wanted the workshops, so there was a pre-interest on their part. It is, nonetheless, a large group from many types of settings (urban/rural) from all quarters of the country.

Responses were classified into themes that were mentioned by a large numbers of participants. Under "obstacles," eight themes were identified:

1. Lack of trust in teachers
2. Lack of confidence/knowledge
3. League tables and inspection
4. Lack of time
5. Overload and lack of coherence
6. Fostered dependency
7. Leadership
8. Loss of what has been gained.

All entries are verbatim quotes. (LEA is local government (district) administrative staff, PHT is primary head teacher (principals), SHT is secondary head teacher, and T is teacher.)

1. *Lack of trust in teachers*
   - Lack of trust of teachers by governments/public/media (LEA)
   - Lack of confidence in the teaching profession (LEA)
   - Government's attitude to teachers and the resulting low esteem and low morale (PHT)
   - Lack of trust from central government (PHT)
   - Those "prescribing" must be seen to listen to those with "professional judgment" (SHT)
   - Lack of trust due to track record (PHT)
   - Trust on the part of government in teachers' skills, motivation, standards, judgment (PHT)
   - Poor morale/lack of public respect and affirmation (T).

2. *Lack of confidence/knowledge/training*
   - Lack of teacher knowledge — training deficit (LEA)
   - To make an "informed" professional judgment you need to be informed (LEA)
   - There would appear to be a considerable range in teachers' skills and knowledge. For the skilled and knowledgeable they are already moving to professional judgment; for others it will provide the excuse to drop those areas where they felt least confident and competent (LEA)
   - Lack of risk-taking culture (PHT)
   - Staff lacking confidence to use their initiative (SHT)
   - Making sure professional judgment is informed, i.e., avoiding reflecting in a vacuum (PHT)
   - Lack of investment in training and development (T)
   - Understanding about the meaning and use of assessment data (LEA)
   - Subject knowledge is lacking (LEA)
   - Lack of the big picture — it's part of informed teaching and learning (SHT)
   - Lack of shared ownership on the part of teachers, due partly to lack of knowledge and skills (T)
   - More staff development needed so teachers feel equipped to take part in the debate (T)
   - Bringing teachers out of their comfort zone (T)
   - Teachers do not fully understand or appreciate the principles, values, and vision behind externally prescribed action/strategies. This leads to blind following of the prescription (PHT)
   - A lack of underpinning knowledge and/or confidence to move forward (PHT).

3. *League tables and inspection*
   - OFSTED (national inspection agency) inspections (LEA)

- Fear of doing it wrong, particularly with impending OFSTED assessment (LEA)
- Removal of "threat" posed by league tables which has a negative impact on open learning culture (PHT)
- To exercise professional judgment involves risk-taking — but the structures of league tables, OFSTED don't encourage this. You need to be brave to innovate in today's climate (LEA)
- Domination of tests/league tables (PHT)
- League tables — schools compete rather than work together and share good practice (T)
- League tables make schools concentrate on "quick fixes" rather than embedded change (LEA)
- We want to improve, not get defensive. Informed professional judgment will come with self-evaluation — the government will have to step back and allow us to take hold of this (SHT).

4. *Lack of time*
   - Lack of time to reflect (T)
   - Not enough time to support colleagues in school in their development (PHT)
   - Lack of opportunity to share good practices which does develop the literacy and numeracy strategies (T)
   - Lack of time within the school day or during INSET (in-service) to reflect/modify practice alongside colleagues (T)
   - Lack of time and energy to plan, evaluate and reflect on practice and its effects (PHT)
   - Lack of teacher time for professional debate leading to improved practice embedded in teachers' belief and commitment (PHT)
   - Quality time for teachers to understand and develop own strategies within government strategy (T)
   - The absence of forums for professional debate (T)
   - Is there space enough to engage critically with informed prescription? There are few teachers to challenge the extent of the informedness (LEA)
   - Lack of time for joint reflection in institutions, across institutions, and across the LEA (LEA)
   - More opportunities and time for practicing teachers to put forward views in a reflective/coherent way and from which information can be gathered which is relevant to the different stages (PHT)
   - Lack of time to develop professionally in order to make good judgments (PHT)

- Time to evaluate, review and plan, time for professional judgment and follow-through (SHT).

5. *Overload and lack of coherence*
   - Innovation fatigue! Lack of clarity of how range of innovations can complement each other in a whole school curriculum model (SHT)
   - The vast range of demands placed on teachers from paperwork to parents, from SATs to social work (SHT)
   - Inability of "change agents" to communicate the bigger picture (PHT).

6. *Fostered dependency*
   - Over-prescription has led to teachers who have little confidence in their own judgment and are not used to thinking critically (LEA)
   - "Learned helplessness" — an over-reliance on the strategies without identifying additional learning opportunities (T)
   - Over-reliance on prescribed materials — provides security and reassurance (LEA)
   - Many young teachers now only know prescription throughout training (SHT)
   - De-skilling of teachers with informed prescription has made the move to professional judgment difficult (PHT)
   - Culture of prescription very strong, especially amongst younger teachers (SHT)
   - Lack of experience of people/teachers in particular who have been told what to do — have little experience thinking and therefore using professional judgment (PHT).

7. *Lack of leadership*
   - Leadership that does not plan for and manage "continuous professional judgment" (T)
   - Shortage of teachers and their recruitment problem (SHT)
   - Poor, uninformed leadership (PHT)
   - Leadership — having the process driven by someone who inspires confidence (PHT).

8. *Loss of what has been gained* (in the informed prescription period)
   - Level of monitoring/feedback/expert intervention may decline (PHT)
   - Dangers of teachers who have "used" the strategies by the book will not have developed the skills and will slip back to uninformed professional judgment (PHT)
   - Fear that results will drop if change is implemented (PHT).

Not a bad list of the major themes. The first two groups (lack of trust and lack of confidence/knowledge) are two sides of the same coin. They capture the Catch 22 dilemma. We would like to trust teachers to have the knowledge, skills, and motivation for effective improvement, but in many cases they don't have these. We are not yet talking about strategy, but we are beginning to get a notion that the strict labels — informed prescription and informed professional judgment — are limited. More about this in a moment.

League tables (publishing achievement results by school and district) and inspection also represent a dilemma. The public thirst for transparency calls for open information about performance; data and the corresponding inspections can be too narrow from the point of view of schools, and/or create a climate of fear or dependency. In England, the punishing nature of OFSTED inspections has lessened a great deal in the last two years. Still, league tables are being published and expected by the public. I would not say that league tables should be dropped (at least not dropped suddenly) in a culture that is used to them. Increasing the capacity to work with league tables is the first order of business. Later, perhaps, they will fade in importance (as, for example, when capacity increases).

Lack of time, as expected, is a key theme. It is encouraging to note that the respondents are not asking for time to be left alone as individuals. The time requests mostly have to do with opportunity to interact, debate, and develop. Of course, the question was about "informed professional judgment." In any case, respondents took to the theme of lack of interaction as an obstacle to development. We see here one potential key to addressing the first two themes of trust/knowledge.

The final four groups of themes also fit in. The sense of overload and problems of coherence discourages teachers from believing that the conditions for professional judgment could be realized. I suspect that it is not overload *per se* that is the culprit but that the bigger problems are fragmentation, lack of ownership, lack of knowledge and skill, and few opportunities to forge greater coherence.

The next theme is related to what I have labeled "fostered dependency." Teachers and leaders possibly read more prescription than actually exists within the literacy and numeracy strategies. This is understandable given league tables and, until recently, a negative inspection system. I also think that the lower the capacity of teachers, the more dependent they could become on seeking external direction. Particularly worrisome are the comments from several respondents that such dependency is the only culture that young teachers have ever known. All the more reason, then, for moving on strategies that push for interactive, cumulative, collective professional judgment. The same is true for leadership. The cycle of dependency and/or lack of ownership cannot be broken without a major investment in leadership development at all levels in the system, and reaping the benefits of attracting and retaining a high quality teaching force (which of course will require implementing the three policy sets discussed in this chapter).

Finally, the fear of losing what has been gained sharpens the problem of treating the two themes of prescription and autonomy too simplistically. The gains in literacy and numeracy have been accomplished through a great deal of hard work at all levels of the system. The edge of order suggests that we maintain the tension between informed prescription (and it doesn't have to be prescribed narrowly) and informed professional judgment as we move forward. In effect, this means envisaging the development of professional judgment as a disciplined process in which external ideas and standards interact with those of local educators. Let's now see what strategies our 600 respondents have in mind.

The strategies, as might be expected, tend to be the flip-side of the obstacles. Five broad themes were identified:

1. Self review/action research
2. Networking and collaboration
3. Training, time
4. Leadership
5. Government action.

1. *Self review/action research*

- Working in partnerships that are involved in self-reviews and reflection (LEA)
- Working alongside teachers, encouraging action research, sharing good practice (LEA)
- Supported school self review (PHT)
- Greater focus on professional skill development and self-monitoring/review of quality (LEA)
- Identifying good practice but not prescriptively — data analysis, evaluation, expertise (T)
- Spread case studies showing how moving away from prescription can work in some circumstances (T)

- Higher profile and commitment to action research thereby raising status of school-based evaluation (LEA)
- Problem-solving opportunities for professionals at different levels to engage in the process of considering professional judgment and its impact (PHT).

2. *Networking/collaboration*

- Dissemination of advice, mentoring, and networking with peers and actual ongoing monitoring and evaluation (LEA)
- Supportive leadership at LEA and school level collaboration at head level through conferences and networks (LEA)
- Teachers observing other teachers and discussing observations (PHT)
- Developing culture of informed professional commitment and understanding. Really can only come about through stronger collaboration between and within schools and spans the professional roles of officers, heads, teachers, and support staff. A tall order, but essential (LEA)
- Practitioners with skills and commitment to change, working with, and for, those reluctant to change (PHT)
- Groups of heads/schools meeting in local "thinktanks" to inspire, encourage and share ideas (PHT)
- Provide opportunity for clustering across schools at frequent intervals and for feedback within schools (T)
- More work at area level to promote the concept of professional learning communities and to combat isolationism (T)
- Growth of collaborative school evaluation (clustered networks of schools and LEA) with achievement of all our children at the center (LEA)
- Identification and sharing of good practice — relying on professional colleagues in schools who are moving forward to spread the message to other schools (LEA)
- Bring small group of practitioners together to renew/plan/act/evaluate and to highlight and spread further the good practice which develops. Tie this to the developing performance management system (SHT)
- More interaction between higher education and primary education — the lack of cooperation and contact, notwithstanding some success stories, is nothing short of scandalous (PHT)

- Given financial means — increased opportunities for mutual observation and a particular observation of those exercising greater skills/judgment (PHT)
- More time and resources for staff to meet, discuss, reflect, share practice, observations both within our school and neighboring schools (PHT)
- Encourage thinking strategically — developing awareness/understanding other schools, sharing good practice, developing team feeling, broaden teachers' perspectives to see the wide/big picture (PHT)
- Networking within schools both inside our own LEA and outside our LEA will develop strengths and understanding and will develop a stronger, more informed voice to engage in debate with the government (PHT).

3. Training/Time

- Good quality training and profession dialogue essential (PHT)
- Exposure to knowledge to increase confidence (books, collaborative working, training) (PHT)
- Performance management at its best provides opportunity for dialogue, coaching, trying out, therefore building belief in professional judgment (LEA)
- Teachers learning to be more confident with data, soft and hard, and see problems as points for inquiry not blame (LEA)
- Understanding of the use of data at an individual level to inform pupil learning at a group level to look at the impact on narrowing the gap between highest and lowest achievers (T)
- Provide time/resources/trainers for teachers and administrators to engage with ideas, methods, packages, that can move their confidence and skills forward (T)
- They need to develop confidence and ownership, i.e., be able to analyze data effectively, determine curricular targets and then adjust planning and teaching in light of this information (LEA)
- More teacher time required to reflect on good practice and to work with colleagues in developing a learning culture (PHT)
- Reconstruct the school day to allow for "intellectual" activity — planning, reviewing (LEA)
- Many teachers have not yet fully implemented the literacy strategy and as yet I am unwilling to "move on" to a more open professional model until all the staff are proficient at the basic skills and techniques of literacy (PHT).

4. *Leadership*

- Management/leadership training to middle managers encourages risk-taking with accountability (LEA)
- Developing support for leadership skills in LEAs, so that they in turn can support schools (LEA)
- Key role of LEA staff to take the lead in introducing, supporting, sustaining the initiatives (SHT)
- Give heads the bottom line imperative that their principal function is as instructional leaders (PHT)
- Development of team leadership skills (T)
- Inspirational leadership and teachers not afraid to take risk, i.e., a risk-taking "can do" culture (PHT)
- Promote the role of the head teacher as a lead professional of a learning community (SHT)
- Head teacher should be linked to other head teachers to plan joint ways forward (PHT).

5. *Government*

- Concentrated and systematic government action to create new climate (SHT)
- Clear national statements that this [moving to informed professional judgment] is the intention (LEA)
- Tackling present perceptions of overload/initiatives and recruitment and retention of staff (LEA)
- Government confidence in its teachers — not just rhetoric (SHT)
- Visible involvement of teachers in developing strategy (T)
- A national teaching council which speaks for the whole profession is represented by the whole profession and which articulates a powerful message of professionalism and idealism. It is not about union issues (LEA)
- Awareness-raising activities relating to national issues/priorities and suggestions on how these may be tackled — based on recent research. These need to be activities that would facilitate discussion and problem-solving (LEA)
- Allow teachers time and input to see the bigger picture, provide support to enable them to become adept at changing plans, to suit the needs of pupils and make best use of human and practical resources (LEA)

- Raise the status of the teaching profession and its cultural value system within the national picture — so that professional judgment is seen as good rather than bad (T)
- Less emphasis on league tables (PHT)
- Using teachers as researchers to inform government policy (PHT)
- Provide systems that cut out some of the donkey work. Teachers spend too much time thinking about/carrying out low-level tasks (PHT)
- You have to convince policymakers it won't lead to anarchy (LEA)
- Create school forums for professional judgment to feed government strategy (PHT)
- Link bottom-up/top-down innovation more explicitly to show where/what we are doing in our own setting fits with the bigger picture (PHT)
- Addressing seriously the issue around morale, workload and recruitment/retention (SHT)
- Celebration of success, interaction, increasingly with other establishments, valuing the gradually growing trust by government of the professionals in the schools (SHT).

The five themes do not add up to a complete plan for introducing greater, informed professional judgment into the reform equation. They were, after all, generated on the spot by local educators in about half an hour (albeit, stimulated by a day-long workshop). The responses, in any case, are encouraging. Teachers, principals, and district staff recognize the need for intensive training and capacity-building. They are more than willing to engage in collaboration at all levels if given some resources to do so. They are open to being led and see the importance of connecting to others and to the big picture. Not all. These are generalizations but there is enough critical mass of interest and ideas to work on the professional capacity and informed judgment agenda. We appear well beyond the uninformed professional judgment era of "leave us alone to teach." Let me be clear, the solution lies in developing, mobilizing and taking advantage of the authority, voice and insight of teachers, heads, and LEA staff.

This could be the time to say a word about technology. It may seem strange that a book on change forces has not mentioned technology. This is no accident. Technology is powerful, but only in the service of a powerful conception. On the one hand, I agree with the wag who said "the teacher who fears he or she will be replaced by computers should be." On the other hand, technology as a solution is overrated. How many resources have been squandered by purchasing technology as if *it* were the innovation? Not so. In the good-to-great companies, Collins (2001) and his colleagues could barely bring themselves to write a chapter on technology even though their preconceptions told them "there must be a technology chapter" (p. 159). As they put it:

> We were quite surprised to find that fully 80 percent of the good-to-great executives we interviewed didn't even mention technology as one of the top five factors in the transition. Furthermore, in the cases where they did mention technology it had a median ranking of fourth with only two executives of 84 interviewed ranking it number one. (p. 155)

Collins and his team conclude, rightly, that we should treat "technology as an accelerator not a creator of momentum" (p. 152). Certainly technology can be a potent servant in enabling collaborative interactions within and across many levels as well as serving as a direct support for teaching and learning. Technology needs to be a central component of any government's investment, but it should play a supporting role.

In any case, the question is how can a government move in the direction of informed professional judgment? It seems to me that any plan must include at least the following:

- A deep conception of what is meant by informed professional judgment
- A clear, public value statement that endorses this direction
- A variety of strategies that create opportunities for teachers to learn and that create disciplined collective action
- A firm commitment to providing resources in a *quid pro quo* manner (quality reform gets more resources)
- An invitation to the profession to engage in dialogue and problem-solving about how to implement this new direction in an accountable, energizing manner to recreate the teaching profession.

To illustrate further we can see elements of the nature of this direction in recent speeches by the two ministers responsible for education in England. The title of a major speech by the Secretary of State for Education and Skills, Estelle Morris, in November 2001 says it best: "Professionalism and Trust — The future of teachers and teaching." We saw earlier the six characteristics of the modern teaching profession outlined in her speech (high standards, a strong body of knowledge and training, efficient organization and use of support staff, leading edge technology, incentives and rewards, and a focus on pupils and parents). The minister states:

> The Government accepts that teachers need more time during the work week to plan, train, think and prepare. And that managers need more time too for their responsibilities in leading schools effectively ... Supporting schools and teachers with the right level of resources is, of course, critical. But we should be clear that this is not just an issue of tackling teachers' workloads, important though that is. It is a much bigger issue, a "something for something" change, whereby we use these resource levels to support the transformation of schools and teaching. (Morris, 2001)

A year later, the minister reaffirms her commitments and expectations for radical reform including a major new focus on secondary schools. In June 2002, she notes:

- Too many pupils [are] going backwards from 11–14 [years of age]
- The link between social class and attainment [is] both strong and worsening between 11 and 16
- Huge variation in standards across schools
- Huge variation in standards within schools. (Morris, 2002a)

Speaking about secondary schools, the minister observes:

> It is time to step up the pace of change. And I say this not because I want to stir things up, or to be on people's backs. It is not because I believe in change for change's sake. I say it because the scale of the challenge is so large, and the need is so great. (Morris, 2002a)

Like many of us around the world, the minister has concluded that we need simultaneously to change *the structure* and *the culture* of our secondary schools, while, by comparison, the main changes in elementary schools have appropriately focused on reculturing first and now, latterly, attention is turning to the restructuring that will be necessary to improve the working and learning conditions of teachers and principals. This is not the place to talk about the substance of reform in high schools, but clearly we will need all of our complexity theory wits about us to tackle secondary school reform.

In a separate speech, Estelle Morris announced additional spending:

[A] record £12.8 billion increase in education spending in England over the next three years will help fund a radical reform of the comprehensive system and a dramatic rise in secondary school standards ...

Spending on education in England will rise by an average of 6 per cent a year in real terms over the next three years, from £45.0 billion in 2002–3 to £57.8 billion in 2005–6. The Spending Review proves that education is the Government's top priority. Investment has risen year on year but investment will be matched by radical reform. We must deliver a secondary education system that delivers higher standards, better behaviour, and more choice. Investment alone will not transform secondary schools. (Morris, 2002b)

As we go to press Estelle Morris suddenly resigned as minister, once again demonstrating the unpredictability of complexity theory. There is no reason to believe that the new Minister, Charles Clarke, will do anything but pursue the same agenda.

Recently, the Minister of State for School Standards, David Miliband, spoke to the National Association of Headteachers Conference. Among other things he said:

We are in the middle of the most sustained increase in education funding in our country's history, by this year amounting to an average increase since 1997 of £680 per pupil in real terms.

The tests results, however much we need value-added tables, and we do, however much we need broader measures of school effectiveness, and we do, show that England ... has one of the fastest improving education systems. The message is clear, reform built on best practice, reform properly funded, reform delivered in partnership, reform aiming for stretching targets, reform that harnesses the energy of pupils and parents as well as teachers can and does work. Estelle Morris has said that investing in teachers and teaching is the top departmental priority for the Spending Review ... It is a unique opportunity to build our education system around the core professional tasks of teaching and learning ...

Reform is about finishing programmes not starting them, and piling behind successful programmes, so we get the full benefit of them; reform is above all, about strengthening the capacity of teachers to teach and students to learn.

You want more investment, so do I. You want higher standards, so do I. But the public wants reforms to ensure their money is well spent. Deliver the reform and they will deliver the funds. Offer them more of the same and they will turn away. (Miliband, 2002)

When it comes to large-scale, sustainable reform, money follows success as much as it precedes it.

Of course, these are political speeches so I reiterate: policymakers have to conceptualize it, say it, mean (value) it, do it, and do more of it. At least in the case of England they are working on the third policy set of improving the quality of the teaching force and the circumstances under which they work. They are at the very early stages of these developments so the plans are incomplete, and it is too early to tell how far they will go. But it is a start well worth watching.

While this chapter has focused on policymakers, the tri-level argument across Chapters 4 to 6 is that the responsibilities are mutual and interactive. Elmore (2002b:5) captures this:

> Accountability must be a reciprocal process. For every increment of performance I demand from you, I have an equal responsibility to provide you with the capacity to meet the expectation. Likewise, for every investment you make in my skill and knowledge, I have a reciprocal responsibility to demonstrate some new increment in performance. This is the principal of "accountability for capacity"
>
> ...
>
> If the public and policymakers want increased attention to academic performance the quid pro quo is investing in the knowledge and skill necessary to produce it. If educators want legitimacy, purpose, and credibility for their work, the quid pro quo is learning to do their work differently and accepting a new model of accountability.

This has been a heavy chapter because the state's agenda is complex, encompassing all three levels. The good news is that there is more action at the level of the state than ever before. In carrying out this agenda, complexity theory encourages us to believe in the power of interacting systems guided by moral purpose and best knowledge. One key ingredient for doing this went missing in the 1990s — the fostering and development of *leadership* at all levels of the system.

Chapter 7

Leadership and Sustainability

My learning curve went straight up.

Anonymous teacher leader

What "standards" were to the 1990s, "leadership" is to the 2000s. This is a natural progression of complexity theory. Standards have only minor leverage over system change. It is "horizon #1". System transformation is different. It can't be accomplished without making leadership at all levels of the system pivotal. This is going to be difficult because we are starting in a hole, and we are losing scores of talented people as demographics change and early retirements increase. This, of course, also provides an opportunity for new leaders, but the volume is such that we will need to devote massive attention to the leadership "problem."

The beauty of complexity theory is that once a system starts to work intensively on an issue it can amplify, and feedback on itself. Not quite the butterfly effect, but perhaps just as magical once it reaches a critical mass.

Fortunately, there is significant conceptual and empirical work underway as people converge on the question of figuring out leadership under dynamically complex conditions. This is a moving target, but I will try to portray where we are. I first take up the nature of new leadership which will give us a good overall feel for what we are talking about. Second, I enter the swamp of what this type of leadership might look like on a day-to-day basis. Third, I consider the cause and effect conditions for developing new leadership on a large scale. It will be no surprise that the learning experiences for leaders will have to be at least as intense and ongoing as that of teachers which we talked about in earlier chapters. In the course of this chapter it will become clear that we are ultimately talking about creating the conditions for sustainability. Sustainability involves transforming the system in a way that the conditions and capacity for continuous improvement become built-in within and across the tri-levels of reform (Chapters 4–6).

We have inherited an irony. The farther you move up the leadership ladder, the less likely you are to engage in purposeful learning for yourself. Thus, it wasn't too long ago that we had to insist that school principals be "in the room" when teachers were receiving new training, or that superintendents had to learn more than how to get the next job. Or that CEOs needed personal coaching and training as part of a team more than anyone. All this is changing for the better. First, the overall nature of leadership is becoming clearer and more exciting, albeit of the daunting variety.

The new nature of leadership

As said earlier, we have made strides during what I called Phase I reform. In this period, mainly the 1990s, we learned how to improve literacy and numeracy at the elementary school level in which the school principal was the key player. Some school districts have become very disciplined in focusing on the development and support of the school principal as instructional leader (Fink and Resnick, 2001).

I also made the case that this will not get us to the next horizon. The principal as instructional leader is too narrow a concept to carry the weight of the kinds of reforms that we need for the future. We need, instead, leaders who can create a fundamental transformation in the learning cultures of schools and the teaching profession itself.

It is more than this. We need leaders who are this good operating at all three levels of the tri-level reform, which means that leaders must be highly effective within their level, *and* in interactions with other levels. Recall that ongoing interaction within and across levels is a fundamental premise of complexity theory (and correspondingly of system transformation). Put still another way, as the three policy sets in Figure 6.2 develop, we need leaders who will be adept at working within the policies, practices, and associated interaction that will evolve. The more sophisticated the system, the more sophisticated the leader.

One step in the direction of defining fundamental leadership is *Leading in a Culture of Change* (Fullan, 2001b). In comparing leaders from successful educational organizations with those from successful businesses, I found a strong convergence between the two. School systems have an edge on moral purpose (but only an edge), while businesses have an advantage in focusing on knowledge development and sharing and on expectations of excellence. But these are differences of degree. Essentially leaders across all organizations had a set of core mind and action sets. These findings are captured in Figure 7.1.

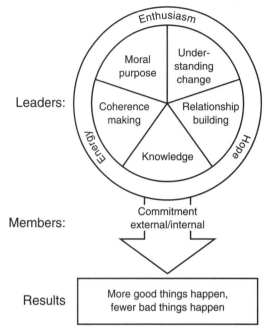

Figure 7.1 Leading in a culture of change (Fullan 2001b)

I won't reiterate the details here, but the short version is that leaders in effective organizations have a constellation of personal factors which I identified as hope (unwarranted optimism), enthusiasm, and energy. They don't have to be born with these. One's vitality can be sapped or enhanced by the conditions under which one works or lives. In any case, these leaders tend to engage others with their energy and are, in turn, energized by the activities and accomplishments of the group.

In addition, I identified five action/mind sets which, it will be no surprise, are congruent with complexity theory. Effective leaders combine a strong sense of moral purpose, an understanding of the dynamics of change, great emotional intelligence as they build relationships, a commitment to new knowledge development and sharing, and a capacity for coherence making (enough coherence on the edge of chaos to still be creative).

Leading in a Culture of Change is accurate as far as it goes, but because the leadership we are talking about is so complex, and so full of details, we need additional takes on its nature. One compatible contribution, because it fleshes out the relationship domain, is Dan Goleman's work on emotional intelligence in leaders and organizations

(Goleman et *al.*, 2002). Goleman and his colleagues talk about the importance of "resonant" leaders who, because of their emotional intelligence, develop "in sync" relationships with and among those in the organization: "they form an emotional bond that helps them stay focused even amid profound change and uncertainty" (Goleman *et al.*, 2002:21).

Goleman then consolidates his work on emotional intelligence into four main domains — two under personal competence, and two under social competence:

Personal competence
- Self-awareness
- Self-management

Social competence
- Social awareness
- Relationship management (p. 39)

In total there are 18 specific competences that cut across the four domains. I won't go into details here, but Goleman and his colleagues emphasize that the competences are not innate, but are "learned abilities." In essence, he found that emotionally intelligent people and leaders live better and more effectively in complex times. I won't say that they live more peacefully (see the swamp section) but they can handle more uncertainty, and conflict, and are better at working through complex issues in a way that ends up energizing rather than depleting the commitment of organizational members.

Of specific interest to us is the research by Goleman and colleagues that focuses on leadership which drew on the database of McBer and Company (now the Hay Group) in a sample of 3,871 executives from Europe, North America, Africa, Australia, and the Pacific Rim. The database focused on leadership style, and its impact on organizational climate, and financial and related performance of the company. Six leadership styles were identified: visionary, coaching, affiliative, democratic, pacesetting, and commanding.

To oversimplify somewhat, Goleman *et al.* found: first, that four of the styles (visionary, coaching, affiliative, democratic) were more associated with positive impact on climate and on performance; second, that leaders had to be good at all four drawing on them differentially across people and situations (put another way, to be only visionary, or only affiliative, etc. is a liability); third, that pacesetting (try to keep up with me), and commanding (do as I say) leaders might have a short-term positive impact under certain conditions, but that they fail sooner than later because they demotivate people, i.e., they do not develop capacity and commitment.

The goal, of course, is to develop organizations whose leaders and members operate with greater emotional intelligence. This is re-culturing of the highest order. We will consider some of the conditions for doing this in the third section of this chapter, and yes, it is going to require tremendous re-learning (and perhaps deep therapy for some of us). But improving emotional intelligence of the individual and the group can be done, and is part and parcel of sustainable reform.

Continued work by the Hay Group is also compatible and instructive. In one study in England which examined the leadership characteristics of 100 highly successful leaders in business with 100 highly successful head teachers, Hay found that both sets of leaders had a lot in common: "head teachers perform well, both in comparison to their counterparts in private business and against the expectations of staff" (Hay Management Consultants, 2000:3). These groups were by selection, the top end of the scale, but it is important to note that leading schools is, if anything, more challenging than leading businesses.

Hay Management Consultants (2000) identified five characteristics of effectiveness, namely: teamwork and developing others; drive and confidence; vision and accountability; influencing tactics and politics; thinking styles (the big picture). All familiar territory to us.

The one area that was most difficult to carry out for both business and education leaders was developing and sustaining *teamwork*, which takes us to another major contribution, this time from Richard Hackman. Having studied teams across airline crews, symphony orchestras, and multiple business organizations, Hackman (2002) concluded that not only does the leader have to be enormously sophisticated about team development, but there also must be certain conditions in place for effectiveness to transpire.

"Effective work teams," Hackman (2002:28) says, "operate in ways that build shared commitment, collective skills, and task-appropriate coordination strategies — not mutual antagonisms and trails of failure from which little is learned." He then delves into the five conditions that he and his colleagues found were required for teams to be effective over time:

> The likelihood of effectiveness is increased when a team (1) is a *real team* rather than a team in name only, (2) has a *compelling direction* for its work, (3) has an *enabling structure* that facilitates

rather than impedes teamwork, (4) operates within a *supportive organizational context*, and (5) has available ample *expert coaching* in teamwork. (Hackman, 2002:31, emphasis in original)

A word about each. Real teams have four features — a team task, clear boundaries, clearly specified authority, and membership stability over some reasonable time (p. 41). A compelling direction is our moral purpose. It is an inspiring goal that has the potential for energizing, orienting, and engaging the team. He cautions that words are not enough: "A team's purpose actually have to *be* challenging [energizing], clear [orients], and consequential [engages]" (p. 72, author's emphasis).

The third condition is an enabling structure which refers to the design, norms of conduct and composition of the team. Design includes defining tasks, enough autonomy to feel responsible, and feedback on the work itself. For norms, Hackman says "keep it simple, but powerful and have only two primary norms":

> 1. Members should take an active, rather than a reactive, stance toward the environment in which the team operates, continuously scanning the environment and inventing or adjusting their performance strategies accordingly ...

> 2. The behavioral boundaries within which the team operates should be demarcated, identifying the small handful of things that members must always do and those they must never do. (p. 106)

Secondary norms, like punctuality, listening and so on, he says are up to the group; they are preferable, but not the main ones for substantial effectiveness. Anticipating our swamp section, Hackman observes,

> The two core norms are unnatural, and the behaviors they support often raise rather than lower anxieties within a work team. And that, in the final analysis is why they usually must be explicitly and deliberately created as part of the team's structure. (p. 112)

Team composition is also complicated. Hackman says avoid "the more the better," don't assume that homogeneity (people getting along) is better, and don't assume that individual and group skills will evolve on their own. As a rule of thumb, Hackman suggests no more than six members. The issue of how a team relates to the rest of the organization is something that Hackman does not dwell on and is obviously critical. Making the team larger does not solve this problem.

For me, the answer in schools, for example, lies in the team learning to develop the school as an organization (Chapter 4) as part of the tri-level transformation agenda.

The first three conditions — real team, compelling direction, enabling structure — are "internal" team matters. The remaining two are "external" — supportive organization context, and expert coaching:

> Features of the organization context, as well as the coaching behaviors of team leaders, can either make it much easier for a team to exploit the advantages of a good basic structure or so powerfully impede the team that the advantages of a fine basic design are negated ... what is needed for team effectiveness is good design *reinforced by* a supportive organization context and expert team coaching. (p. 133, author's emphasis)

Supportive context concerns the reward and accountability system, information systems, technical assistance, resources — all things familiar to us from earlier chapters. It is, in a word, Elmore's (2002b) accountability principle of reciprocity.

Finally, expert coaching is for individuals on the team as well as for the team as a group. Hackman stresses that the focus of coaching must be on "a team's task, processes and outcomes, not on members' social interactions or interpersonal relationships" (p. 192). He is talking about primary focus, and is clearly not against interpersonal competencies. I think he is right, as he takes us a step closer to the swamp, that interpersonal harmony is not what we want at the heart of complexity transformation, that interpersonal difficulties are sometimes a symptom rather than a cause of poor performance, and that:

> ... research shows that certain patterns of interaction that often are experienced as problematic by team members and coded the same way by outside observers actually can promote team performance and member learning ... task-based conflict is one such pattern, and the vocal presence of a member with "deviant" views is another. (pp. 193–4)

The scarcity of skilled coaches who are this good (who know, for example, when "to leave things alone and let the tensions remain high for a while" (p. 194) is of course, another matter that must be addressed. Chicken and egg problems abound in complexity theory by definition because most change forces are both a cause and an effect as systems interact.

All of this is to conclude with Hackman's fundamental contribution:

Both practicing managers and writers about management commonly view the actions of leaders as "causes" and the response of teams as "effect." In cause-effect models, particular leader behaviors and styles are viewed as strongly determining team behavior and performance. By contrast, I view the main responsibility of leaders as creating and maintaining the five conditions that increase the chances that a team will, over time, become increasingly effective in carrying out its work. (Hackman, 2002:31)

Complexity theory could not have said it better. There is more to the nature of leadership, but for that we have to enter the swamp.

Leading in the swamp

The characteristics of effective leadership are not what they seem. They do not involve creating harmonious groups; inspiring charismatic leadership is a liability; and even pursuing emotional intelligence as an end in itself can lead to superficial first horizon change. The edge of chaos is a more swamp-like than terra firma because it is at the heart of complexity's dynamism. A few examples enable us to go deeper into the nature of leadership.

The first is from the Hay Group in an intriguing exploratory study of "maverick" head teachers in England (Hay Group Management Ltd., 2002). This research focused on a select group of ten heads of schools who had done something dramatic or impressive in achieving extraordinary results in their schools. Five, in particular, had achieved what the report called "breakthrough results." Hay cautions that it is an exploratory, small-scale study, and I use it not to advocate what they found but as an entry point to the swamp.

Six themes emerged from the study which they describe as follows:

1. *Crossing the line*
   How far can you go before "questioning assumptions" becomes breaking the rules? Is it even right to cross this line?
2. *Taking risks*
   Breakthrough leaders risk their careers and their reputations for their principles. Should they ask other people to risk theirs?
3. *Connected thinking*
   Breakthrough leaders are creative but not original — they seek out ideas that already work and make them fit their context.
4. *Making enemies*
   If politics is the art of compromise, why is stubbornness so persuasive?

5. *The business of learning*

    Is enterprise a dirty word? People who care about education care about money.

6. *Sharing leadership*

    When heads spend so much time looking outward, who looks after the school? (Hay Group Management Ltd., 2002:3)

We see a few links to complexity theory such as taking risks, working on connected thinking, and developing shared leadership within the team. Moreover, the breakthrough leaders were strong on two components of leadership that most principals find most difficult, namely, "holding people accountable," and "coaching and developing staff."

But there are also question marks: these leaders sometimes run roughshod over people who get in their way; they have little interest in the agenda of other levels of the system; they aren't particularly collaborative except within their own schools. They aren't replicable (which might be a good thing).

More to the point, the behaviors of these leaders may have arisen because of the inadequacies of the larger "system" more than anything. And that is my conclusion. The weakness of the present systems to foster and reward breakthrough leaders causes some heads to become deviant. It may be necessary, and it may be useful for their schools for a while, but it won't improve the system, and the leaders themselves won't benefit from becoming even more effective if the larger system was actually a help rather than an obstacle.

A more thorough study of leadership by Heifetz and Linsky (2002) allows us to experience the swamp much more productively. *Leadership on the Line: Staying Alive Through the Dangers of Leading* gives us a good idea of what we are in for. Recall from Chapter 1 that Heifetz and Linsky make a key distinction between "technical" challenges in which we apply current know-how and can be led top-down, and "adaptive challenges," which require us to learn new ways (the solution isn't known) and must be eventually carried out by the people with the problem. Quite a good distinction actually between "horizon #1" and "horizon #2" which we also discussed in Chapter 1.

The problem is that if it involves learning brand new ways, *and* if people must own the solution, people are going to have to do things that they don't have the capacity to do. Leaders, in other words, have to lead people through a process of doing something that they are not (at the outset) particularly good at, and don't want to do — or at least don't want to pay the price — anxieties, losses, etc. — of so doing. This is what makes it swampy.

Remember we are talking about something that has never been done before — transformative changes in the way people act and learn. Heifetz and Linsky (2002:2–3) set the stage:

> Each day brings you opportunities to raise important questions, speak to higher values and surface unresolved conflicts. Every day you have a chance to make a difference in the lives of people around you.
>
> And every day you must decide whether to put your contribution out there, or keep it to yourself to avoid upsetting anyone, and get through another day. You are right to be cautious. Prudence is a virtue. You disturb people when you take up unpopular initiatives in your community, put provocative new ideas on the table in your organization, question the gaps between colleagues' values and behavior, or ask friends and relatives to face up to tough realities. You risk people's ire and make yourself vulnerable. Exercising leadership can get you into a lot of trouble ...
>
> [But] leadership is worth the risk because the goals extend beyond material gain or personal advancement. By making the lives of people around you better, leadership provides meaning in life. It creates purpose.

If you go too far as a leader you risk being "marginalized" by authorities, "diverted," "attacked," and so forth. Heifetz and Linsky suggest five main responses for staying the course in working through adaptive challenges, and still staying alive as a leader. The first they call "Get on the balcony." This means gaining perspective on the problem, linking to the bigger picture, and periodically stepping back from the action. It involves trying to be in two places at once — in the midst of action and above it:

> Leadership is an improvisational art. You may have an overarching vision, clear, orienting values, and even a strategic plan, but what you actually do from moment to moment cannot be scripted ... To be effective you have to respond to what is happening. Going back to our metaphor, you have to move back and forth from the balcony to the dance floor, over and over again throughout the day, week, month, and year. You take action, step back and assess the results of action, reassess the plan, then go to the dance floor and make the next move. You have to maintain a diagnostic mindset on a changing reality ...
>
> Sustaining your leadership, then, requires first and foremost the capacity to see what is happening to you and your initiative, as it is happening. (p. 73)

"Think politically" is the second theme, and one that we saw earlier in the Hay Management Consultants list. This involves establishing relationships with all, but especially with those you disagree with. This is why surrounding yourself with people who agree with you is fatal. Being empathetic, learning from those who oppose you, accepting responsibility for your limitations, acknowledging the loss of others, modeling new behavior, and accepting casualties are all part of this theme. Incidentally, a good test of your empathy is to try and accurately convey to others the viewpoints of someone you disagree with on an important issue who is "not in the room."

"Accepting casualties" also deserves comment. Heifetz and Linsky say that casualties (people leaving the organization because of lack of fit) are often "a necessary by-product of adaptive work" (p. 100). Collins (2001) makes a strong case for getting the right people "on the bus" (and the wrong people off the bus). It is critical, for example, to have the right people in leadership positions across the organization. But two cautions. One, these actions are in the context of other values which commit to developing people and to respecting deviant opinions. Second, we have to be especially careful in school systems that we don't pass the casualties around. Our tri-level argument is that *all* schools must improve so that the overall system context becomes strong. You don't do this by having a few good buses.

The third theme is "orchestrate the conflict." It can sound and be quite manipulative, but it is a key theme of complexity theory. The edge of chaos is that place where anxiety to do something is high enough that it can be addressed, but not so high that chaos erupts. All the advice we have marshaled about deep change in this book is consistent on this point. All change worth its salt involves anxiety and conflict, and resisting the urge to paper it over is critical … Leaders, in other words, sometimes need to raise the temperature, and other times, control it. Heifetz and Linsky suggest that leaders can constructively raise the temperature in two ways:

> First, bring attention to the hard issues, and keep it focused there. Second, let people feel the weight of responsibility for tackling those issues. Conflicts will surface within the relevant groups as contrary points of view are heard. (p. 109)

Lowering the temperature, when needed, might involve stepping back and addressing small problems, temporarily reclaiming responsibility for tough issues, slowing down the pace and process of challenging norms and expectations. Leaders, according to Heifetz and Linsky, have to take the temperature of the group constantly.

Theme four, "give the work back" is the bane of charismatic and pacesetting leaders because if things are moving too slowly they take over and attempt to provide the solution or do the work:

> By trying to solve adaptive challenges for people, at best you will reconfigure it as a technical problem and create short-term relief. (Heifetz and Linsky, 2002:123)

Capacity-building as we defined it earlier is about giving people the training, resources, and opportunity to pursue complex tasks, and then to hold them accountable. Leaders have "to think constantly about giving the work back to the people who need to take the responsibility" (p. 139).

The final theme is "hold steady!" Taking the heat, and not panicking in the face of conflict is one aspect, as is the patience to what Heifetz and Linsky call "letting the issue ripen" — or perhaps fostering the ripening process. As they observe, "an issue becomes ripe when there is widespread urgency to deal with it" (p. 146). And, "the lack of knowledge on an issue is almost always in direct proportion to its lack of ripeness" (p. 151). Thus, for example, capacity-building which focuses on moral purpose, skills, knowledge about achievement gaps and what can be done about them might all be thought of as part of the ripening process where people's sense of passion, commitment and know-how reach a breakthrough point.

Further evidence that the swamp is more revealing than we might have thought is contained in Badaracco's (2002) study of *Leading Quietly*. Quiet leaders are:

> ... people who choose responsible, behind-the-scenes action over public heroism to resolve tough leadership challenges. These individuals don't fit the stereotype of the bold and gutsy leader, and they don't want to. What they want is to do the "right thing" for their organizations, their co-workers, and themselves — inconspicuously and without casualties. They do so by being boldly realistic about the complexities of their own motives and those of the dilemmas they face. (Badaracco, 2002, book cover)

In a series of case studies, Badaracco illustrates how quiet leaders resolve big problems by "a long series of small efforts [which] despite its slow pace, often turns out to be the quickest way to make an organization — and the world — a better place" (p. 2). Taking us through the swamp ("messy everyday challenges"), Badaracco makes the case that quiet leaders: "don't kid themselves"; "trust mixed motives" in themselves and others (self-interest and altruism run together); "buy a little time" in the face of complex challenges; "invest wisely" their political capital; "drill down" into complex problems; "bend the rules without breaking them" ("they do this after grappling with the complexities of a situation, not as a shortcut around them" (p. 126); "nudge, test and escalate gradually" ("Instead of a problem–solution paradigm, they rely on an act–learn–act–learn approach" and "craft a compromise by avoiding either or thinking and looking for both/and outcomes" (p. 128).

Clearly these are capacities that you don't learn from a recipe book, but because they are better suited to the real complexity of organizations they point to how we should and should not approach leadership development (more about this shortly).

Similar ideas are portrayed by Farson and Keyes (2002). Although the title of their book engaged in hyperbole (*Whoever Makes the Most Mistakes Wins*) their main message is sound. "Manage success and failure by not making clear distinctions between the two" they argue (p. 10). They are not the first to say that learning from failure is at least as instructive as learning from success. Indeed, "success is at least as hazardous as failure. It means redefining our sense of self around being a success rather than an unfinished portrait" (p. 47). Again they are not the first to observe that treating success as a destiny results in emptiness once we get there. In the world of complexity there are always new horizons: "genuine success is not a state but a [never ending] process" (Farson and Keyes, 2002:126).

One final set of attributes cuts across effective leaders which allows them to keep going, swamp and all. All of the in-depth studies found a small number of personal characteristics that were akin to the spiritual (Webster's definition is "a life-giving force") and that gave leaders meaning in life (as Charles Handy (2002:126) observes: "A worthwhile life … requires you to have a purpose beyond yourself"). Different labels were used in the various studies, but they all relate to this spiritual domain.

Badaracco (2002) calls them three quiet virtues: restraint, modesty, and tenacity. Heifetz and Linsky (2002) refer to the three virtues of a "sacred heart" — innocence, curiosity and compassion (and how to avoid losing heart into "cynicism, arrogance, and callousness." Hackman (2002) placed emotional maturity and courage alongside knowledge and know-how. And Jim Collins' (2001:20) leaders in the

11 *Good to Great* built enduring greatness "through a paradoxical blend of extreme personal humility and intense professional will."

As we look back I won't try to summarize the first two sections of this chapter. They are compatible. The first provides an overview of the nature of leadership required for complex times. It is, as it were, like a view from the balcony. We get a good sense of the transformational nature of new leadership, and it is an enormously powerful portrait. Ironically, it would be very easy to take these deep conceptions and implement them superficially. People are always looking for shortcuts and quick fixes to complexity. For that reason learning on the dance floor is just as important as having the bigger picture in mind. The two together — powerful concepts and learning in the swamp — define leadership for complexity.

Cause and effect conditions

What came first, the chicken or the egg? In complexity theory the answer is both. You need great conditions to develop the leaders we have been talking about, and you need great leaders to develop the conditions which will produce the leaders, and so on.

And we are starting in a deep hole. Massive turnover in leadership positions, combined with a neglect (until recently) of policies and strategies for leadership development have, in most places, reached a crisis level (especially if we use the criteria of leadership for complexity discussed in this chapter).

I am not going to review the state of leadership initiatives now underway. Since leadership is *the* strategy of the decade, there are countless research and development activities underway (for an excellent analysis of the state of leadership in North America, see Leithwood *et al.* (in press); for England, see Earley *et al.* (2002)). Instead, I will suggest five interrelated themes that have simultaneous cause/effect properties, that is, they pertain in combination to creating conditions that enhance the chances of *sustainability*.

The themes are: opportunity and depth of learning, policies for individual development, learning in context and systemness, leadership succession and leaders at many levels, and improving the teaching profession. The good news, as our review of research on leadership indicates, is that the characteristics of effective leaders are accessible to most of us. They do not involve heroic leaders, charismatic visionaries or saint-like virtues. Under the right conditions they can be learned. The difficult news is that it is going to require hard work over many years to simultaneously develop leaders and alter conditions.

The first theme — opportunity and depth of learning — is to serve notice that the current system of leadership development provides extremely weak and episodic possibilities of working on the agenda outlined in this chapter and in the book as a whole. All the things that apply to teachers apply in spades to leaders. Overall, then, we need to design and invest in many opportunities for people to engage in learning to lead. The other themes cover some of these: standards and individual development, mentoring and expert coaching, learning in and changing context, and so on. I am going to say that it takes some ten years of purposeful, day-to-day learning on and off the job to become proficient enough to keep on learning and leading. We don't have this now. This chapter shows how very, very much leaders need to know, and how far short we fall in providing the conditions for leader learning.

Second, individual, standards-based development is important. This, in effect, concerns the second policy set in Figure 6.2. Standards for what educational leaders need to know and be able to do, and opportunities for working on these capacities is clearly needed. The National College of School Leadership in England with its focus on the conceptions and skills of school leaders (congruent with section one of this chapter) is one example, as are the standards summarized by Earley *et al.* (2002), and Leithwood *et al.* (in press)).

Third, the work on individual standards will amount to naught if people don't have an opportunity to learn in and help change contexts. For one thing, people need to practice in the swamp with expert mentors and coaches. For another, even if they learn as individuals they won't be influential if the context doesn't change (never send a changed individual into an unchanged environment).

We need, in other words, policies and practices akin to the third policy set from Figure 6.2 — those that are directed at changing the conditions under which leaders learn. Learning with other leaders inside and outside the school is part of this. Although valuable, learning collaboratives which bring people together across schools and districts are insufficient because they do not necessarily meet "the systemness" criterion which is whether some policies and strategies are aimed at altering the culture of school and/or district (Chapters 4 and 5). What this means is that we have to work directly with schools as organizations, and use school districts as local system organizers to create new contexts (led by new context leaders) which do better at student learning precisely *because* they provide better environments for teacher leaders and school leaders to develop in those organizations. All the way up and down the line we are talking about increasing system capacity — the capacity of the district to work with schools, the capacity of the state to work with districts and schools.

Fourth, leaders at many levels and their associated leadership succession need separate attention. If you pursue the first three themes you will produce leaders at many levels, but only if we also pay much more attention to succession. There is no more neglected topic either in research, policy, or practice. In research we should be investigating conditions for successful succession as much as we focus on new leaders and startups. We should be selecting leaders in terms of their capacity to create the conditions of other leaders to flourish and make a continuing impact beyond our terms. In this sense the main mark of successful leaders is not their impact on the bottom line (of profit or student achievement) in the short run, but rather how many effective leaders there are in the organization at the end of their tenures. As Collins (2001:36) found, the good-to-great leaders in his study "channel ambition into the company, not the self; sets up successor for even greater success in the next generation."

Finally, and this brings us full circle, leaders need to help cause improvement in working conditions and development of the teaching profession because this is how great leadership is effected for the future. We will only get quality principals in numbers if we have quality teachers in numbers, because it is from teacher ranks that future leadership derives. This is a virtuous circle because leaders can only go as deep as their organization is capable of.

Over the seven chapters we have taken quite a complex journey. Complexity theory is neutral in that the forces of change can do good or do evil. We know that we cannot "control" complexity, but by understanding better how it works and by using the social attractors we can exploit its enormous natural power. In the course of doing this, guided complexity theory at its best generates, unleashes and puts to great use the energies, passion and commitment of people heaven bent to making a difference and getting more meaning and satisfaction from their daily lives.

It is not so much a matter of going down the road less traveled, but rather going down one never before traveled because it has not yet been made. Travel and make the road. Make the road and travel. The edge of chaos or the edge of order? You pick. And then go for it.

References

AMERICAN INSTITUTES FOR RESEARCH (2002). *Evaluation of the Blueprint for Student Success in a Standards-based System*. Palo Alto, CA: AIR.

BADARACCO, J. (2002). *Leading Quietly*. Boston, MA: Harvard Business School Press.

BAKER, P., CURTIS, D. and DENENSON, W. (1991). *Collaborative Opportunities to Build Better Schools*. Bloomington, IL: Illinois Association for Supervision and Curriculum Development.

BARBER, M. (2001). "Large-scale education reform in England." Paper prepared for the School Development Conference, 25–26 October, Tartu University, Estonia.

BARBER, M. (2002). "From Good to Great: Large-scale Reform in England." Paper presented at Futures of Education conference, April 23, Universität Zürich, Zürich.

BENNETT, N., ANDERSON, L. and WISE, C. (2002). "School–LEA partnerships: recipe for success or chimera." Paper presented at the American Educational Research Association annual meeting, 1–5 April, New Orleans.

BERENDS, M., BODILLY, S. and KIRBY, S. (2002). *Facing the Challenge of Whole-School Reform*. Santa Monica, CA: RAND.

BLOCK, P. (2002). *The Answer to How is Yes*. San Francisco, CA: Berrett-Koehler.

BRANSFORD, J., BROWN, A. and COCKING, K. (eds) (1999). *How People Learn: Bridging Research and Practice*. Washington, DC: National Academy Press.

BRICKER, D. and GREENSPON, E. (2001). *Searching for Certainty*. Toronto: Doubleday.

BROWN, J. and DUGUID, P. (2000). *The Social Life of Information*. Boston, MA: Harvard Business School Press.

CALIFORNIA COMMISSION ON TEACHER CREDENTIALING (1997). *California Standards for the Profession*. Sacramento, CA: California Commission on Teacher Credentialing.

COHEN, D. and HILL, H. (2001). *Learning Policy: When State Education Reform Works*. New Haven, CT: Yale University Press.

COLLINS, J. (2001). *Good to Great*. New York, NY: HarperCollins Publishers.

DARLING-HAMMOND, L. (2002). "Building instructional quality." Paper presented at the American Educational Research Association annual meeting, 1–5 April, New Orleans.

DICEMBRE, E. (2002). "How they turned the ship around." *Journal of Staff Development*, Spring, 32–5.

DRYDEN, K. (1995). *In School*. Toronto: McClelland & Stewart Publications.

EARL, L., LEVIN, B., LEITHWOOD, K., FULLAN, M. and WATSON, N. (2003). *England's National Literary and Numeracy Strategies: Final Report*. London: Department for Education and Skills.

EARLEY, P., EVANS, J., COLLARBONE, P., GOLD, A. and HALPIN, D. (2002). *Establishing the Current State of School Leadership in England*. London: Department for Education and Skills.

EDGE, K., ROLHEISER, C. and FULLAN, M. (2001). "Case studies of literacy-driven educational change: The Toronto District School Board's Early Years Literacy Project." Toronto: Ontario Institute for Studies in Education, University of Toronto. Unpublished report.

EDGE, K., ROLHEISER, C. and FULLAN, M. (2002). "Case studies of assessment literacy-driven change: Edmonton Catholic Schools." Toronto: Ontario Institute for Studies in Education, University of Toronto. Unpublished report.

ELMORE, R. (2002a). "Hard questions about practice." *Educational Leadership* (59)8: 22–5.

ELMORE, R. (2002b). *Bridging the Gap between Standards and Achievement.* Washington, DC: Albert Shanker Institute.

ELMORE, R. (2003). "The problem of stakes in performance-based accountability systems. In S. FUHRMAN and R. ELMORE (eds) *Redesigning Accountability Systems.* New York: Teachers College Press.

ELMORE, R. and BURNEY, D. (1999). "Investing in teacher learning." In L. DARLING-HAMMOND and G. SYKES (eds) *Teaching as the Learning Profession*, 236–91. San Francisco, CA: Jossey-Bass.

FARSON, R. and KEYES, R. (2002). *Whoever Makes the Most Mistakes Wins.* New York, NY: The Free Press.

FINK, E. and RESNICK, L. (2001). "Developing principals as instructional leaders." *Phi Delta Kappan.* 82: 598–606.

FRANCESCHINI, L. (2002). "Memphis, what happened? Notes on the decline and fall of comprehensive school reform." Paper presented at the American Educational Research Association annual meeting, 1–5 April, New Orleans.

FULLAN, M. (1993). *Change Forces: Probing the Depths of Educational Reform.* London: Falmer Press.

FULLAN, M. (1997). *What's Worth Fighting for in the Principalship?* 2nd edn. New York, NY: Teachers College Press.

FULLAN, M. (1999). *Change Forces: The Sequel.* London: Falmer Press.

FULLAN, M. (2001a). *The New Meaning of Educational Change.* 3rd edn. New York, NY: Teachers College Press.

FULLAN, M. (2001b). *Leading in a Culture of Change.* San Francisco, CA: Jossey-Bass.

FULLAN, M. (in press). *The Moral Imperative of the Principalship.* Thousand Oaks, CA: Corwin Press, Toronto: Ontario Principals Council.

FULLAN, M. and HARGREAVES, A. (1992). *What's Worth Fighting For in Your School.* New York, NY: Teachers College Press.

GALBRAITH, J.K. (2002). "Stop the madness." *Toronto Globe and Mail*, July 6, p. 38.

GLADWELL, M. (2000). *The Tipping Point.* Boston, MA: Little, Brown & Company.

GLEICK, J. (1999). *Faster: The Acceleration of Just About Everything.* New York: Pantheon Books.

GOLEMAN, D., BOYATZIS, R. and MCKEE, A. (2002). *Primal Leadership.* Boston, MA: Harvard Business School Press.

HACKMAN, R. (2002). *Leading Teams.* Boston: Harvard Business School Press.

HANDY, C. (2002). *The Elephant and the Flea.* London: Hutchinson.

HARGREAVES, A. (2003). *Teaching in the Knowledge Society.* New York, NY: Teachers College Press.

HARGREAVES, A. and FULLAN, M. (1998). *What's Worth Fighting for Out There?* New York, NY: Teachers College Press.

HARGREAVES, D. (2002). "Policy levers." Paper presented on policy reform at invitational meeting, March, Department for Education and Skills, London.

HATCH, T. (2002). *What happens When Multiple Improvement Initiatives Collide?* Menlo Park, CA: Carnegie Foundation for the Advancement of Teaching.

HAY GROUP MANAGEMENT LTD. (2002). *No Barriers, No Boundaries: Breakthrough Leadership that Transforms Schools.* London: Hay Group Management.

HAY MANAGEMENT CONSULTANTS (2000). *The Lessons of Leadership.* London: Hay Management Consultants.

HEIFETZ, R. and LINSKY, M. (2002). *Leadership on the Line: Staying Alive Through the Dangers of Leading.* Boston, MA: Harvard Business School Press.

HESS, F. (1999). *Spinning Wheels: The Politics of Urban School Reform.* Washington, DC: Brookings Institute.

HIGHTOWER, A. (2002). "San Diego's big boom: system instructional change in the central office and schools." In A. Hightower, M. Knapp, J. Marsh and M. McLaughlin (eds) *School Districts and Instructional Renewal*, 115-145. New York, NY: Teachers College Press.

HIGHTOWER, A., KNAPP, M., MARSH, J. and McLAUGHLIN, M. (eds) (2002). *School Districts and Instructional Renewal.* New York, NY: Teachers College Press.

HOBAN, G. (2002). *Teacher Learning for Educational Change.* Buckingham: Open University Press.

KEATING, D. and HERTZMAN, C. (eds) (1999). *Developmental Health and the Wealth of Nations.* New York, NY: The Guilford Press.

KHURANA, R. (2002). *Searching for a Corporate Savior: The Irrational Quest for Charismatic CEOs.* Boston, MA: Harvard Business School Press.

LEITHWOOD, K., JANTZI, D. and STEINBACH, R. (in press). "Leadership practices for accountable schools." In K. LEITHWOOD and P. HALLINGER (eds) *Second International Handbook of Educational Leadership and Administration.* Dordecht: Kluwer Press.

LIVSEY, R., with PALMER, P. (1999). *The Courage to Teach: A Guide to Reflection and Renewal.* San Francisco: Jossey-Bass.

LORTIE, D. (1975). *School Teacher: A Sociological Study.* Chicago, IL: University of Chicago Press.

McLAUGHLIN, M. and TALBERT, J. (2001). *Professional Communities and the Work of High School Teaching.* Chicago, IL: University of Chicago Press.

MARION, R. (1999). *The Edge of Organization.* Thousand Oaks, CA: Sage Publishers.

MASCALL, B., FULLAN, M. and ROLHEISER, C. (2001). "The challenges of coherence and capacity." Toronto: The Ontario Institute for Studies in Education, University of Toronto. Unpublished report.

MILIBAND, D. (2002). Speech to National Head Teachers conference 6 June, Torquay. Available online at http://www.naht.org.uk/themes/campaign-item-view.asp?ID=207&sid=22.

MORRIS, E. (2001). "Professionalism and trust — the future of teachers and teaching." Speech to the Social Market Foundation, 12 November, London: Social Market Foundation.

MORRIS, E. (2002a). "Comprehensive school reform." Speech to the Social Market Foundation, 24 June, London: Social Market Foundation. Available online at http://www.smf.co.uk/Speeches.html.

MORRIS, E. (2002b). "Spending review." (Speech), 15 July, London: Department for Education and Skills.

NEWMANN, F., KING, B. and YOUNGS, P. (2000). "Professional development that addresses school capacity." Paper presented at the American Educational Research Association annual meeting, 1–5 April, New Orleans.

NEW AMERICAN SCHOOLS (2002). *A Decade of Experience*. Arlington, VA: New American Schools.

OECD (2000). *Knowledge and Skills for Life: First Results from PISA 2000*. Paris: Organization for Economic Cooperation and Development.

PALMER, P. (1998). *The Courage to Teach*. San Francisco, CA: Jossey-Bass.

PRICEWATERHOUSECOOPERS (2001). *Teacher Workload Study*. London: Department for Education and Skills.

ROTHSTEIN, R. (2002). "Out of balance: our understanding of how schools affect society and how society affects schools." 30th Anniversary Essay, Chicago: The Spencer Foundation.

SAN DIEGO CITY SCHOOLS DISTRICT (2000). *Blueprint for student success in a standards-based system*. San Diego, CA: San Diego City Schools District.

SAUL, J. (1997). *Reflections of a Siamese Twin*. London: Penguin Books.

SHIELDS, P., HUMPHREY, D., WECHSLER, M., RIEHL, L., TIFFANY-MORALES, J., WOODWORTH, K., VIKI, M. and PRICE, T. (2001). *The Status of The Teaching Profession, 2001*. Santa Cruz, CA: The Center for the Future of Teaching and Learning.

SNYDER, J. (2002). "New Haven Unified School District." In A. HIGHTOWER, M. KNAPP, J. MARSH and M. MCLAUGHLIN (eds) *School Districts and Instructional Renewal*, 146–75. New York, NY: Teachers College Press.

SOBER, E. and WILSON, D. (1998). *Unto Others: The Evolution and Psychology of Unselfish Behavior*. Cambridge, MA: Harvard University Press.

SPILLANE, J. (2002). "District policymaking and state standards." In A. HIGHTOWER, M. KNAPP, J. MARSH and M. MCLAUGHLIN (eds) *School Districts and Instructional Renewal*, 228–77. New York, NY: Teachers College Press.

STACEY, R. (1992) *Managing the Unknowable*. San Francisco, CA: Jossey-Bass.

STACEY, R. (1996). *Complexity and Creativity in Organizations*. San Francisco, CA: Berrett-Koehler.

STACEY, R. (2001). *Complex Responsive Processes in Organizations*. London: Routledge.

STEIN, M., HUBBARD, L. and MEHAN, H. (2002). "Reform ideas that travel far afield: the two cultures of reform in New York City's District 2 and San Diego." Paper presented at the American Educational Research Association annual meeting, 1–5 April, New Orleans.

WENGER, E., MCDERMOTT, R. and SNYDER, W. (2002). *Cultivating Communities of Practice*. Boston, MA: Harvard Business School Press.

WILMS, D. (2001). "Monitoring school performance for 'standards-based reform'." *Evaluation and Research in Education* 14: 1–20.

WILSON, S., DARLING-HAMMOND, L. and BERRY, B. (2001). *A Case of Successful Teaching Policy: Connecticut's Long-term Efforts to Improve Teaching and Learning*. Seattle, WA: Center for the Study of Teaching and Policy, University of Washington.

Index